THE CRIMINAL LAW AND THE CRIMINAL PROCEDURE LAW OF THE PEOPLE'S REPUBLIC OF CHINA

中华人民共和国刑法
中华人民共和国刑事诉讼法

FOREIGN LANGUAGES PRESS   BEIJING

First Edition   1984

ISBN 0-8351-1015-X

Published by the Foreign Languages Press
24 Baiwanzhuang Road, Beijing, China

Printed by the Foreign Languages Printing House
19 West Chegongzhuang Road, Beijing, China

Distributed by China International Book
Trading Corporation (Guoji Shudian),
P.O. Box 399, Beijing, China

Printed in the People's Republic of China

PUBLISHER'S NOTE

China has long had a considerable body of individual statutes and regulations on criminal law and procedure. However, it was not until 1979 that the People's Republic of China enacted her first comprehensive codes of law in these fundamental areas. The two laws represent the distillation of years of debate and practical experience, and form an essential basis for China's effort to establish a sound socialist legal system.

The present volume includes translations of the Criminal Law and Criminal Procedure Law as well as several subsequent decisions that amend or supplement the two laws to reflect particular problems such as the rise in economic crime. The English translations contained in this volume are not authorized by official quarters. Therefore, the Chinese originals must be referred to in case of doubt as to interpretation.

The translations of the two laws have appeared in similar form in the U.S. *Journal of Criminal Law and Criminology*, Spring 1982.

The translators are Jerome A. Cohen, American lawyer and former Professor of Law and Director of East Asian Legal Studies, Harvard Law School, U.S.A., Timothy A. Gelatt, B.A., University of Pennsylvania, J.D., Harvard Law School, now an

American lawyer in Hong Kong, and Florence M.L. Li, S.J.D., Harvard Law School, collaborating with Mr. Cohen on studies of Chinese law.

Various associates of Messrs. Cohen and Gelatt are to be thanked for their contributions, including Alexandra Tod who assisted with the Glossaries.

CONTENTS

目　　录

The Criminal Law of the People's Republic of
  China   5
中华人民共和国刑法   65

The Criminal Procedure Law of the People's
  Republic of China   111
中华人民共和国刑事诉讼法   169

Appendices:
附录：

Decision of the Standing Committee of the
  National People's Congress Regarding the
  Question of Approval of Cases Involving
  Death Sentences   217
全国人民代表大会常务委员会关于死刑案件核准
  问题的决定   219

Decision of the Standing Committee of the National People's Congress Regarding the Handling of Offenders Undergoing Reform Through Labour and Persons Undergoing Re-

habilitation Through Labour Who Escape or
Commit New Crimes 220

全国人民代表大会常务委员会关于处理逃跑或者
重新犯罪的劳改犯和劳教人员的决定 224

Decision of the Standing Committee of the National People's Congress Regarding the Question of the Time Limits for Handling Criminal Cases 226

全国人民代表大会常务委员会关于刑事案件办案
期限问题的决定 228

Decision of the Standing Committee of the National People's Congress Regarding the Severe Punishment of Criminals Who Seriously Undermine the Economy 229

全国人民代表大会常务委员会关于严惩严重破坏
经济的罪犯的决定 234

Decision of the Standing Committee of the National People's Congress Regarding the Severe Punishment of Criminal Elements Who Seriously Endanger Public Security 241

全国人民代表大会常务委员会关于严惩严重危害
社会治安的犯罪分子的决定 243

Decision of the Standing Committee of the National People's Congress Regarding the Procedure for Rapid Adjudication of Cases Involving Criminal Elements Who Seriously Endanger Public Security 246

全国人民代表大会常务委员会关于迅速审判严重危害社会治安的犯罪分子的程序的决定	248
Decision of the Standing Committee of the National People's Congress Regarding the Exercise by the State Security Organs of the Public Security Organs' Powers of Investigation, Detention, Preparatory Examination and Carrying out Arrest	250
全国人民代表大会常务委员会关于国家安全机关行使公安机关的侦查、拘留、预审和执行逮捕的职权的决定	251
English-Chinese Glossary 英汉词汇对照表	252
Chinese-English Glossary 汉英词汇对照表	273

THE CRIMINAL LAW OF THE PEOPLE'S REPUBLIC OF CHINA

(Adopted by the Second Session of the Fifth National People's Congress, July 1, 1979 and Effective as of January 1, 1980)

CONTENTS

PART I GENERAL PROVISIONS 9

  Chapter I Guiding Ideology, Tasks and Scope of Application of the Criminal Law 9

  Chapter II Crimes 12
    Section 1 Crimes and Criminal Responsibility 12
    Section 2 Preparation for a Crime, Criminal Attempt and Discontinuation of a Crime 15
    Section 3 Joint Crimes 16

  Chapter III Punishments 17
    Section 1 Types of Punishments 17
    Section 2 Control 19
    Section 3 Criminal Detention 20
    Section 4 Fixed-term Imprisonment and Life Imprisonment 20
    Section 5 The Death Penalty 21
    Section 6 Fines 22
    Section 7 Deprivation of Political Rights 23
    Section 8 Confiscation of Property 24

  Chapter IV The Concrete Application of Punishments 25
    Section 1 Sentencing 25
    Section 2 Recidivists 26
    Section 3 Voluntary Surrender 27
    Section 4 Combined Punishment for More Than One Crime 27
    Section 5 Suspension of Sentence 28
    Section 6 Reduction of Sentence 30
    Section 7 Parole 30
    Section 8 Limitation 31

  Chapter V Other Provisions 32

PART II SPECIAL PROVISIONS 35

  Chapter I Crimes of Counterrevolution 35

Chapter II	Crimes of Endangering Public Security	39
Chapter III	Crimes of Undermining the Socialist Economic Order	42
Chapter IV	Crimes of Infringing Upon the Rights of the Person and the Democratic Rights of Citizens	47
Chapter V	Crimes of Property Violation	52
Chapter VI	Crimes of Disrupting the Order of Social Administration	54
Chapter VII	Crimes of Disrupting Marriage and the Family	60
Chapter VIII	Crimes of Dereliction of Duty	62

PART I GENERAL PROVISIONS

CHAPTER I GUIDING IDEOLOGY, TASKS AND SCOPE OF APPLICATION OF THE CRIMINAL LAW

Article 1 The Criminal Law of the People's Republic of China, which takes Marxism-Leninism-Mao Zedong Thought as its guide and the Constitution as its basis, is formulated in accordance with the policy of combining punishment with leniency and in light of actual circumstances and the concrete experiences of all of our country's ethnic groups in carrying out the people's democratic dictatorship led by the proletariat and based on the worker-peasant alliance, that is, the dictatorship of the proletariat, and in conducting socialist revolution and socialist construction.

Article 2 The tasks of the Criminal Law of the People's Republic of China are to use criminal punishments to struggle against all counterrevolutionary and other criminal acts in order to defend the system of the dictatorship of the proletariat, to protect socialist property owned by the whole people and property collectively owned by the labouring masses, to protect citizens' lawful privately-owned property, to protect citizens' rights of the person, democratic rights and other rights, to maintain social order, order in production, order in work, order in education and scientific research and order in the lives of the masses of people, and to safeguard the smooth progress of the cause of socialist revolution and socialist construction.

Article 3 This Law is applicable to all who commit crimes within the territory of the People's Republic of China except as specially stipulated by law.

This Law is also applicable to all who commit crimes aboard a ship or airplane of the People's Republic of China.

When either the act or consequence of a crime takes place within the territory of the People's Republic of China, a crime is to be deemed to have been committed within the territory of the People's Republic of China.

Article 4 This Law is applicable to citizens of the People's Republic of China who commit the following crimes outside the territory of the People's Republic of China:

1. Crimes of counterrevolution;

2. Crimes of counterfeiting national currency (Article 122) and counterfeiting valuable securities (Article 123);

3. Crimes of corruption (Article 155), accepting bribes (Article 185) and disclosing state secrets (Article 186); and

4. Crimes of posing as state personnel to cheat and bluff (Article 166) and forging official documents, certificates and seals (Article 167).

Article 5 This Law is also applicable to citizens

of the People's Republic of China who commit crimes outside the territory of the People's Republic of China other than the crimes specified in the preceding article, provided that this Law stipulates a minimum sentence of not less than a three-year fixed term of imprisonment for such crimes; but an exception is to be made if a crime is not punishable according to the law of the place where it was committed.

Article 6 This Law may be applicable to foreigners who, outside the territory of the People's Republic of China, commit crimes against the state of the People's Republic of China or against its citizens, provided that this Law stipulates a minimum sentence of not less than a three-year fixed term of imprisonment for such crimes; but an exception is to be made if a crime is not punishable according to the law of the place where it was committed.

Article 7 Any person who commits a crime outside the territory of the People's Republic of China and according to this Law should bear criminal responsibility may still be dealt with according to this Law even if he has been tried in a foreign country; however, a person who has already received criminal punishment in a foreign country may be exempted from punishment or given a mitigated punishment.

Article 8 The problem of the criminal responsibility of foreigners who enjoy diplomatic privileges and immunity is to be resolved through diplomatic channels.

Article 9 This Law is to become effective on January 1, 1980. If an act committed after the founding of the People's Republic of China and before the implementation of this Law was not deemed a crime under the laws, decrees and policies at that time, the laws, decrees and policies at that time are to be applicable. If the act was deemed a crime under the laws, decrees and policies at that time, and if under the provisions of Chapter IV, Section 8, of the General Provisions of this Law it should be prosecuted, criminal responsibility is to be investigated according to the laws, decrees and policies at that time. However, if this Law does not deem it a crime or imposes a lesser punishment, this Law is to be applicable.

CHAPTER II CRIMES

SECTION 1 CRIMES AND CRIMINAL RESPONSIBILITY

Article 10 All acts that endanger the sovereignty and territorial integrity of the state, endanger the system of the dictatorship of the proletariat, undermine the socialist revolution and socialist construction, undermine social order, violate property owned by the whole people or property collectively owned by the labouring masses, violate citizens' lawful privately-owned property, infringe upon citizens' rights of the person, democratic rights and other rights, and other acts that endanger society are crimes if according to law they should be criminally punished; but if the circumstances are clearly minor and the harm is not great, they are not to be deemed crimes.

Article 11 An intentional crime is a crime constituted as a result of clear knowledge that one's own act will cause socially dangerous consequences, and of hope for or indifference to the occurrence of those consequences.

Criminal responsibility shall be borne for intentional crimes.

Article 12 A negligent crime occurs when one should foresee that one's act may cause socially dangerous consequences but fails to do so because of carelessness or, having foreseen the consequences, readily assumes he can prevent them, with the result that these consequences occur.

Criminal responsibility is to be borne for negligent crimes only when the law so stipulates.

Article 13 Although an act objectively creates harmful consequences, if it does not result from intent or negligence but rather stems from irresistible or unforeseeable causes, it is not to be deemed a crime.

Article 14 A person who has reached the age of sixteen who commits a crime shall bear criminal responsibility.

A person who has reached the age of fourteen but not the age of sixteen who commits the crimes of killing another, serious injury, robbery, arson, habitual theft, or other crimes seriously undermining social order shall bear criminal responsibility.

A person who has reached the age of fourteen but not the age of eighteen who commits a crime shall be given a lesser punishment or a mitigated punishment.

When a person is not punished because he has not reached the age of sixteen, the head of his family or guardian is to be ordered to subject him to discipline. When necessary, he may also be given shelter and rehabilitation by the government.

Article 15 A mentally ill person who causes dangerous consequences at a time when he is unable to recognize or unable to control his own conduct is not to bear criminal responsibility; but his family or guardian shall be ordered to subject him to strict surveillance and arrange for his medical treatment.

A person whose mental illness is of an intermittent nature shall bear criminal responsibility if he commits a crime during a period of mental normality.

An intoxicated person who commits a crime shall bear criminal responsibility.

Article 16 A deaf-mute or a blind person who commits a crime may be given a lesser punishment or a mitigated punishment or be exempted from punishment.

Article 17 Criminal responsibility is not to be borne for an act of legitimate defence that is undertaken to avert present unlawful infringement of the public interest or the rights of the person or other rights of the actor or of other people.

Criminal responsibility shall be borne where legitimate defence exceeds the necessary limits and causes undue harm. However, consideration shall be given according to the circumstances to imposing a mitigated punishment or to granting exemption from punishment.

Article 18 Criminal responsibility is not to be borne for an act of urgent danger prevention that cannot but be undertaken in order to avert the occurrence of present danger to the public interest or the rights of the person or other rights of the actor or of other people.

Criminal responsibility shall be borne where urgent danger prevention exceeds the necessary limits and causes undue harm. However, consideration shall be given according to the circumstances to imposing a mitigated punishment or to granting exemption from punishment.

The provisions of the first paragraph with respect to preventing danger to oneself do not apply to a person who bears specific responsibility in his post or profession.

SECTION 2 PREPARATION FOR A CRIME, CRIMINAL ATTEMPT AND DISCONTINUATION OF A CRIME

Article 19 Preparation for a crime is preparation of the instruments or creation of the conditions for the commission of a crime.

One who prepares for a crime may, in comparison with one who consummates the crime, be given a lesser punishment or a mitigated punishment or be exempted from punishment.

Article 20 Criminal attempt occurs when a crime has already begun to be carried out but is not consummated because of factors independent of the will of the criminal element.

One who attempts to commit a crime may, in comparison with one who consummates the crime, be given a lesser punishment or a mitigated punishment.

Article 21 Discontinuation of a crime occurs when, during the process of committing a crime, the actor voluntarily discontinues the crime or voluntarily and effectively prevents the consequences of the crime from occurring.

One who discontinues a crime shall be exempted from punishment or be given a mitigated punishment.

SECTION 3 JOINT CRIMES

Article 22 A joint crime is an intentional crime committed by two or more persons jointly.

A negligent crime committed by two or more persons jointly is not to be punished as a joint crime; those who should bear criminal responsibility are to be punished separately according to the crimes they have committed.

Article 23 A principal offender is one who organizes and leads a criminal group in conducting criminal activities or plays a principal role in a joint crime.

A principal offender shall be given a heavier punishment unless otherwise stipulated in the Special Provisions of this Law.

Article 24 An accomplice is one who plays a secondary or supplementary role in a joint crime.

An accomplice shall, in comparison with a principal offender, be given a lesser punishment or a mitigated punishment or be exempted from punishment.

Article 25 One who is coerced or induced to participate in a crime shall, according to the circumstances of his crime, be given a mitigated punishment in comparison with an accomplice or be exempted from punishment.

Article 26 One who instigates others to commit a crime shall be punished according to the role he plays in the joint crime. One who instigates a person under the age of eighteen to commit a crime shall be given a heavier punishment.

If the instigated person does not commit the instigated crime, the instigator may be given a lesser punishment or a mitigated punishment.

CHAPTER III PUNISHMENTS

SECTION 1 TYPES OF PUNISHMENTS

Article 27 Punishments are divided into principal punishments and supplementary punishments.

Article 28 The types of principal punishments are:

1. Control;*

---

* Control (管制) is a criminal penalty imposed for minor offences. The offender continues to work in his place of employment and continues to receive his normal wages, while undergoing the supervision of the public security organs and the masses. He is required to make periodic reports on his circumstances to the public security organ concerned. *See* Arts. 33 and 36 below. *See also* "What Is Control?", *People's Daily*, December 10, 1982. This penalty is often translated in China's English-language publications as "public surveillance". — *Trans.*

2. Criminal detention;*
3. Fixed-term imprisonment;
4. Life imprisonment; and
5. The death penalty.

Article 29 The types of supplementary punishments are:
1. Fines;
2. Deprivation of political rights; and
3. Confiscation of property.

Supplementary punishments may also be applied independently.

Article 30 Deportation may be applied in an independent or supplementary manner to a foreigner who commits a crime.

Article 31 Where the victim has suffered economic loss as a result of a criminal act, the criminal element, in addition to receiving criminal sanction according to law, shall in accordance with the circumstances be sentenced to make compensation for the economic loss.

Article 32 Where the circumstances of a person's crime are minor and do not require sentencing

---

* Criminal detention (拘役) is a criminal penalty imposed for relatively minor offences. The criminal on whom this penalty is imposed is deprived of his freedom and confined in a detention house by the local organ of public security rather than being put in prison or sent to a place of reform through labour as are those serving fixed terms or life sentences. He may go home for one or two days each month and be paid for work. The penalty of criminal detention is not to be confused with *xingshi juliu* (刑事拘留), by which is meant the pre-trial detention employed by the public security organs. *See* Arts. 37-39 below and The Criminal Procedure Law of the People's Republic of China, Arts. 38-52. *See also* "What Is Criminal Detention?", *People's Daily*, December 17, 1982. — *Trans.*

to punishment, an exemption from criminal sanctions may be granted him, but he may, according to the different circumstances of each case, be reprimanded or ordered to make a statement of repentance or formal apology, or make compensation for losses, or be subjected to administrative sanctions by the competent department.

SECTION 2 CONTROL

Article 33 The term of control is not less than three months and not more than two years.

Control is to be decided by judgment of a people's court and executed by a public security organ.

Article 34 A criminal element who is sentenced to control must abide by the following rules during the term in which his control is being carried out:

1. Abide by laws and decrees, submit to the supervision of the masses and actively participate in collective productive labour or work;

2. Report regularly on his own activities to the organ executing the control; and

3. Report and obtain approval from the organ executing the control for a change in residence or departure from the area.

A criminal element who is sentenced to control shall, while engaged in labour, receive equal pay for equal work.

Article 35 Upon the expiration of the term of the control, the organ executing the control shall immediately announce the termination of control to the criminal element sentenced to control and to the masses concerned.

Article 36 The term of control is counted as commencing on the date the judgment begins to be executed; where custody has been employed before the judgment begins to be executed, the term is to be shortened by two days for each day spent in custody.

SECTION 3 CRIMINAL DETENTION

Article 37 The term of criminal detention is not less than fifteen days and not more than six months.

Article 38 A criminal element sentenced to criminal detention is to have his sentence executed by the public security organ in the vicinity.

During the period of execution, a criminal element sentenced to criminal detention may go home for one or two days each month; consideration may be given according to the circumstances to granting compensation to those who participate in labour.

Article 39 The term of criminal detention is counted as commencing on the date the judgment begins to be executed; where custody has been employed before the judgment, the term is to be shortened by one day for each day spent in custody.

SECTION 4 FIXED-TERM IMPRISONMENT AND LIFE IMPRISONMENT

Article 40 The term of fixed-term imprisonment is not less than six months and not more than fifteen years.

Article 41 A criminal element sentenced to fixed-term imprisonment or life imprisonment is to have his sentence executed in prison or in another place for reform through labour; reform through labour is to be carried out on anyone with the ability to labour.

Article 42 The term of fixed-term imprisonment is counted as commencing on the date the judgment begins to be executed; where custody has been employed before the judgment begins to be executed, the term is to be shortened by one day for each day spent in custody.

SECTION 5 THE DEATH PENALTY

Article 43 The death penalty is only to be applied to criminal elements who commit the most heinous crimes. In the case of a criminal element who should be sentenced to death, if immediate execution is not essential, a two-year suspension of execution may be announced at the same time the sentence of death is imposed, and reform through labour carried out and the results observed.

Except for judgments made by the Supreme People's Court according to law, all sentences of death shall be submitted to the Supreme People's Court for approval. Sentences of death with suspension of execution may be decided or approved by a high people's court.*

Article 44 The death penalty is not to be applied

---

* This article has been modified by the Decision of the Standing Committee of the National People's Congress Regarding the Question of Approval of Cases Involving Death Sentences. *See* pp. 217-18 below. — *Trans.*

to persons who have not reached the age of eighteen at the time the crime is committed or to women who are pregnant at the time of adjudication. Persons who have reached the age of sixteen but not the age of eighteen may be sentenced to death with a two-year suspension of execution if the crime committed is particularly grave.

Article 45 The death penalty is to be executed by means of shooting.

Article 46 If a person sentenced to death with a suspension of execution truly repents during the period of suspension, he is to be given a reduction of sentence to life imprisonment upon the expiration of the two-year period; if he truly repents and demonstrates meritorious service, he is to be given a reduction of sentence to not less than fifteen years and not more than twenty years of fixed-term imprisonment upon the expiration of the two-year period; if there is verified evidence that he has resisted reform in an odious manner, the death penalty is be executed upon the order or approval of the Supreme People's Court.

Article 47 The term for suspending execution of a sentence of death is counted as commencing on the date the judgment becomes final. The term of a sentence that is reduced from the death penalty with suspension of execution to fixed-term imprisonment is counted as commencing on the date of the order reducing the sentence.

SECTION 6   FINES

Article 48 In imposing a fine, the amount of

the fine shall be determined according to the circumstances of the crime.

Article 49 A fine is to be paid in a lump sum or in installments within the period specified in the judgment. Upon the expiration of the period, one who has not paid is to be compelled to pay. If a person truly has difficulties in paying because he has suffered irresistable calamity, consideration may be given according to the circumstances to granting him a reduction or exemption.

SECTION 7 DEPRIVATION OF POLITICAL RIGHTS

Article 50 Deprivation of political rights is deprivation of the following rights:

1. The right to elect and the right to be elected;
2. The rights provided for in Article 45 of the Constitution;*
3. The right to hold a position in state organs; and
4. The right to hold a leading position in any enterprise, institution or people's organization.

Article 51 The term of deprivation of political rights is not less than one year and not more than five years, except as stipulated in Article 53 of this Law.

In situations where a person is sentenced to control and to deprivation of political rights as a supple-

---

* This refers to the Constitution adopted on March 5, 1978, which has since been superseded by the Constitution adopted on December 4, 1982. The relevant article of the latter Constitution is Article 35. — *Trans.*

mentary punishment, the term of deprivation of political rights is to be the same as the term of control, and the punishments are to be executed at the same time.

Article 52 A counterrevolutionary element shall be sentenced to deprivation of political rights as a supplementary punishment; when necessary, a criminal element who seriously undermines social order may also be sentenced to deprivation of political rights as a supplementary punishment.

Article 53 A criminal element who is sentenced to death or to life imprisonment shall be deprived of political rights for life.

When the death penalty with a suspension of execution is reduced to fixed-term imprisonment, or life imprisonment is reduced to fixed-term imprisonment, the term of the supplementary punishment of deprivation of political rights shall be changed to not less than three years and not more than ten years.

Article 54 The term of the supplementary punishment of deprivation of political rights is counted as commencing on the date that imprisonment or criminal detention ends or on the date that parole begins; the deprivation of political rights is naturally to be effective during the period in which the principal punishment is being executed.

SECTION 8 CONFISCATION OF PROPERTY

Article 55 Confiscation of property is the confiscation of part or all of the property personally owned by the criminal element.

When a sentence of confiscation of property is imposed, property that belongs to or should belong to family members of the criminal element may not be confiscated.

Article 56 Where it is necessary to use the confiscated property to repay legitimate debts incurred by the criminal element before the property was sealed under court order, the people's court is so to order at the request of the creditors.

CHAPTER IV THE CONCRETE APPLICATION OF PUNISHMENTS

SECTION 1 SENTENCING

Article 57 When deciding the punishment of a criminal element, the sentence shall be imposed on the basis of the facts of the crime, the nature and circumstances of the crime and the degree of harm to society, in accordance with the relevant stipulations of this Law.

Article 58 Where the circumstances of a criminal element are such as to give him a heavier punishment or a lesser punishment under the stipulations of this Law, he shall be sentenced to a punishment within the legally prescribed limits of punishment.

Article 59 Where the circumstances of a criminal element are such as to give him a mitigated punishment under the stipulations of this Law, he shall be sentenced to a punishment below the legally prescribed punishment.

Although the circumstances of a criminal element do not warrant giving him a mitigated punishment under the stipulations of this Law, if, according to the concrete situation of the case, to sentence him to the minimum legally prescribed punishment is still to impose too heavy a punishment, upon decision of the adjudication committee of the people's court he too may be sentenced to a punishment below the legally prescribed punishment.

Article 60 All articles of property illegally obtained by the criminal element shall be recovered or he shall be ordered to make restitution or pay compensation for them. Contraband and the criminal's own articles of property used for committing the crime shall be confiscated.

SECTION 2   RECIDIVISTS

Article 61 A criminal element who has been sentenced to a punishment of not less than fixed-term imprisonment and who, within three years after his punishment has been completely executed or he has received a pardon, commits another crime for which he should be sentenced to a punishment of not less than fixed-term imprisonment is a recidivist and shall be given a heavier punishment. However, negligent commission of a crime is an exception.

In situations where a criminal element is granted a parole, the period stipulated in the preceding paragraph is to be counted as commencing on the date of expiration of the parole.

Article 62 Counterrevolutionary elements who, at

any time after their punishment has been completely executed or they have received a pardon, commit another crime of counterrevolution are all to be treated as recidivists.

SECTION 3 VOLUNTARY SURRENDER

Article 63 Those who voluntarily surrender after committing a crime may be given a lesser punishment. Those among them whose crimes are relatively minor may be given a mitigated punishment or be exempted from punishment; if their crimes are relatively serious, they may also be given a mitigated punishment or be exempted from punishment if they demonstrate meritorious service.

SECTION 4 COMBINED PUNISHMENT FOR MORE THAN ONE CRIME

Article 64 If a person commits more than one crime before judgment has been pronounced, except where he is sentenced to death or life imprisonment, the term of sentence that it is decided to execute, in consideration of the circumstances, shall be less than the total term for all the crimes but more than the maximum term for any of the crimes; however, the term of control cannot exceed three years, the term of criminal detention cannot exceed one year, and fixed-term imprisonment cannot exceed twenty years.

If among the crimes there are any for which a supplementary punishment is to be imposed, the supplementary punishment must still be executed.

Article 65 If after judgment has been pronounced but before the punishment has been completely executed it is discovered that, before judgment was pronounced, the sentenced criminal element committed another crime for which he has not been sentenced, a judgment shall be rendered for the newly-discovered crime, and the punishment to be executed for the punishments sentenced in the two, former and latter, judgments decided according to the stipulations of Article 64 of this Law. The term that has already been executed shall be counted in the term decided by the new judgment.

Article 66 If after judgment has been pronounced but before the punishment has been completely executed the sentenced criminal element again commits a crime, a judgment shall be rendered for the newly-committed crime, and the punishment to be executed for the punishment that has not been executed for the former crime and the punishment imposed for the latter crime decided according to the stipulations of Article 64 of this Law.

SECTION 5 SUSPENSION OF SENTENCE

Article 67 A suspension of sentence may be pronounced for a criminal element who has been sentenced to criminal detention or to fixed-term imprisonment for not more than three years, according to the circumstances of his crime and his demonstration of repentance, and where it is considered that applying a suspended sentence will not in fact result in further harm to society.

If a criminal element for whom a suspension of sentence has been pronounced has been sentenced to a supplementary punishment, the supplementary punishment must still be executed.

Article 68 The probation period for suspension of criminal detention is to be not less than the term originally decided and not more than one year, but it may not be less than one month.

The probation period for suspension of fixed-term imprisonment is to be not less than the term originally decided and not more than five years, but it may not be less than one year.

The probation period for suspension is to be counted as commencing on the date the judgment becomes final.

Article 69 Suspension of sentence is not to be applied to counterrevolutionary criminals or recidivists.

Article 70 A criminal element for whom a suspension of sentence has been pronounced is to be turned over by the public security organ to his unit or to a basic level organization for observation during the probation period for suspension, and, if he commits no further crime, upon the expiration of the probation period for suspension, the punishment originally decided is not to be executed; if he commits any further crime, the suspension is to be revoked and the punishment to be executed for the punishments imposed for the former and latter crimes decided according to the stipulations of Article 64 of this Law.

SECTION 6 REDUCTION OF SENTENCE

Article 71 A criminal element who is sentenced to control, criminal detention, fixed-term imprisonment or life imprisonment may have his sentence reduced if, during the period his punishment is being executed, he truly repents or demonstrates meritorious service. However, for those sentenced to control, criminal detention or fixed-term imprisonment, the term of the punishment actually to be executed may not, after one or more reductions of sentence, be less than half of the term originally decided; for those sentenced to life imprisonment, it may not be less than ten years.

Article 72 The term of fixed-term imprisonment that is reduced from life imprisonment is counted as commencing on the date of the order reducing the sentence.

SECTION 7 PAROLE

Article 73 A criminal element sentenced to fixed-term imprisonment of which not less than half has been executed, or a criminal element sentenced to life imprisonment of which not less than ten years has actually been executed, may be granted parole if he demonstrates true repentance and will not cause further harm to society. If special circumstances exist, the above restrictions relating to the term executed need not be imposed.

Article 74 The probation period for parole in the case of fixed-term imprisonment is the term that has not been completed; the probation period for parole in the case of life imprisonment is ten years.

The probation period for parole is counted as commencing on the date of parole.

Article 75 During the probation period for parole, a criminal element who is granted parole is to be supervised by the public security organs, and, if he commits no further crime, the punishment to which he was originally sentenced is to be considered as having been completely executed; if he commits any further crime, the parole is to be revoked and the punishment to be executed for the punishment that has not been executed for the former crime and the punishment imposed for the latter crime decided according to the stipulations of Article 64 of this Law.

SECTION 8 LIMITATION

Article 76 Crimes are not to be prosecuted where the following periods have elapsed:

1. In cases where the maximum legally-prescribed punishment is fixed-term imprisonment of less than five years, where five years have elapsed.

2. In cases where the maximum legally-prescribed punishment is fixed-term imprisonment of not less than five years and less than ten years, where ten years have elapsed.

3. In cases where the maximum fixed-term imprisonment is not less than ten years, where fifteen years have elapsed.

4. In cases where the maximum legally-prescribed punishment is life-imprisonment or death, where

twenty years have elapsed. If it is considered that a crime must be prosecuted after twenty years, the matter must be submitted to the Supreme People's Procuratorate for approval.

Article 77 No limitation on the period for prosecution is to be imposed in cases where, after the people's courts, people's procuratorates or public security organs have taken coercive measures, the criminal element escapes from investigation or adjudication.

Article 78 The period for prosecution is counted as commencing on the date of the crime; if the criminal act is of a continuous or continuing nature, it is counted as commencing on the date the criminal act is completed.

If any further crime is committed during the period for prosecution, the period for prosecution of the former crime is counted as commencing on the date of the latter crime.

CHAPTER V   OTHER PROVISIONS

Article 79 A crime that is not expressly stipulated in the Special Provisions of this Law may be determined and punished according to the most closely analogous article of the Special Provisions of this Law, but the matter shall be submitted to the Supreme People's Court for approval.

Article 80 In situations where the autonomous areas inhabited by ethnic groups cannot completely apply the stipulations of this Law, the organs of state power of the autonomous regions or of the provinces may formulate alternative or supplementary provisions based upon the political, economic and cultural characteristics of the local ethnic groups and the basic principles of the stipulations of this Law, and these provisions shall go into effect after they have been submitted to and approved by the Standing Committee of the National People's Congress.

Article 81 The "public property" spoken of in this Law refers to the following property:

1. Property owned by the whole people; and
2. Property owned collectively by the labouring masses.

Private property that is being managed, used or transported by the state, people's communes, cooperatives, joint ventures and people's organizations is to be treated as public property.

Article 82 The "citizens' lawful privately-owned property" spoken of in this Law refers to the following property:

1. Citizens' lawful income, savings, houses or other means of livelihood; and
2. Means of production such as reserved plots of land, reserved livestock and reserved trees that are under individual or family ownership or use according to law.

Article 83 The "state personnel" spoken of in this Law refers to all personnel of state organs, enterprises and institutions and other personnel engaged in public service according to law.

Article 84 The "judicial personnel" spoken of in this Law refers to personnel engaged in the functions of investigating, prosecuting, adjudicating and supervising and controlling offenders.

Article 85 The "serious injury" spoken of in this Law refers to any one of the following injuries:

1. Injuries resulting in loss of the use of a person's limbs or in disfigurement;
2. Injuries resulting in loss of a person's hearing, sight or function of any other organ; and
3. Other injuries that cause grave harm to a person's physical health.

Article 86 The "ringleader" spoken of in this Law refers to a criminal element who plays the role of organizing, planning or directing a criminal group or a crowd assembled to commit a crime.

Article 87 "To be handled only upon complaint", spoken of in this Law, refers to handling a case only when the victim brings a complaint. If the victim is unable to bring a complaint because of coercion or intimidation, a people's procuratorate and close relatives of the victim may also bring the complaint.

Article 88 "Not less than", "not more than" and "within", spoken of in this Law, all include the given figure.

Article 89 The General Provisions of this Law are applicable to other laws and decrees with stipulations for criminal punishments, but other laws having special stipulations are exceptions.

PART II SPECIAL PROVISIONS

CHAPTER I CRIMES OF COUNTERREVOLUTION

Article 90 All acts endangering the People's Republic of China committed with the goal of overthrowing the political power of the dictatorship of the proletariat and the socialist system are crimes of counterrevolution.

Article 91 Whoever colludes with foreign states in plotting to harm the sovereignty, territorial integrity and security of the motherland is to be sentenced to life imprisonment or not less than ten years of fixed-term imprisonment.

Article 92 Whoever plots to subvert the government or dismember the state is to be sentenced to life imprisonment or not less than ten years of fixed-term imprisonment.

Article 93 Whoever instigates, lures or bribes state personnel, members of the armed forces, people's police or people's militia to defect to the enemy and turn traitor or to rise in rebellion is to be sentenced to life imprisonment or not less than ten years of fixed-term imprisonment.

Article 94 Whoever defects to the enemy and turns traitor is to be sentenced to not less than three years and not more than ten years of fixed-term imprisonment; when the circumstances are serious or it is a case of leading a group to defect to the enemy and turn traitor, the sentence is to be not less than ten years of fixed-term imprisonment or life imprisonment.

Whoever leads members of the armed forces, people's police or people's militia to defect to the enemy and turn traitor is to be sentenced to life imprisonment or not less than ten years of fixed-term imprisonment.

Article 95 Ringleaders in armed mass rebellion or others involved whose crimes are monstrous are to be sentenced to life imprisonment or not less than ten years of fixed-term imprisonment; other active participants are to be sentenced to not less than three years and not more than ten years of fixed-term imprisonment.

Article 96 Ringleaders in a mass prison raid or in organizing a jailbreak or others involved whose crimes are monstrous are to be sentenced to life imprisonment or not less than ten years of fixed-term imprisonment; other active participants are to be sentenced to not less than three years and not more than ten years of fixed-term imprisonment.

Article 97 Whoever commits any of the following acts of espionage or aiding an enemy is to be sentenced to not less than ten years of fixed-term imprisonment or life imprisonment; when the circumstances are relatively minor, the sentence is to be not less than three years and not more than ten years of fixed-term imprisonment:

1. Stealing, secretly gathering or providing intelligence for an enemy;

2. Supplying arms and ammunition or other military materials to an enemy; and

3. Taking part in a secret service or espionage organization or accepting a mission assigned by an enemy.

Article 98 Whoever organizes or leads a counterrevolutionary group is to be sentenced to not less than five years of fixed-term imprisonment; others who actively participate in a counterrevolutionary group are to be sentenced to not more than five years of fixed-term imprisonment, criminal detention, control or deprivation of political rights.

Article 99†† Whoever organizes or uses feudal superstition or superstitious sects and secret societies to carry on counterrevolutionary activities is to be sentenced to not less than five years of fixed-term imprisonment; when the circumstances are relatively minor, the sentence is to be not more than five years of fixed-term imprisonment, criminal detention, control or deprivation of political rights.

Article 100 Whoever for the purpose of counterrevolution carries on any of the following acts of sabotage is to be sentenced to life imprisonment or not less than ten years of fixed-term imprisonment; when the circumstances are relatively minor, the sentence is to be not less than three years and not more than ten years of fixed-term imprisonment:

1. Causing explosions, setting fires, breaching dikes, using technological or other means to sabotage military equipment, production facilities, communications or transportation equipment, construction

---

†† Articles where this symbol appears have been revised by the Decision of the Standing Committee of the National People's Congress Regarding the Severe Punishment of Criminal Elements Who Seriously Endanger Public Security. *See* pp. 239-40 below. — *Trans.*

projects, danger-prevention equipment or other public construction or articles of public property;

2. Robbing state records, military materials, industrial or mining enterprises, banks, shops, warehouses or other articles of public property;

3. Hijacking ships, airplanes, trains, streetcars, or motor vehicles;

4. Pointing out bombing or shelling targets to the enemy; and

5. Manufacturing, seizing or stealing guns or ammunition.

Article 101 Whoever for the purpose of counterrevolution spreads poisons, disseminates germs or by other means kills or injures people is to be sentenced to life imprisonment or not less than ten years of fixed-term imprisonment; when the circumstances are relatively minor, the sentence is to be not less than three years and not more than ten years of fixed-term imprisonment.

Article 102 Whoever for the purpose of counterrevolution commits any of the following acts is to be sentenced to not more than five years of fixed-term imprisonment, criminal detention, control or deprivation of political rights; ringleaders or others whose crimes are monstrous are to be sentenced to not less than five years of fixed-term imprisonment:

1. Inciting the masses to resist or to sabotage the implementation of the state's laws or decrees; and

2. Through counterrevolutionary slogans, leaflets or other means, propagandizing for and inciting the overthrow of the political power of the dictatorship of the proletariat and the socialist system.

Article 103 Whoever commits any of the crimes

of counterrevolution mentioned above in this Chapter, except those in Articles 98, 99 and 102, may be sentenced to death when the harm to the state and the people is especially serious and the circumstances especially odious.

Article 104 Whoever commits any of the crimes in this Chapter may in addition be sentenced to confiscation of property.

CHAPTER II CRIMES OF ENDANGERING PUBLIC SECURITY

Article 105 Whoever endangers public security by setting fires, breaching dikes, causing explosions or using other dangerous means to sabotage factories, mines, oilfields, harbours, rivers, water sources, warehouses, dwellings, forests, farms, threshing grounds, pastures, important pipelines, public buildings or other public or private property, in cases where serious consequences have not been caused, is to be sentenced to not less than three years and not more than ten years of fixed-term imprisonment.

Article 106 Whoever sets fires, breaches dikes, causes explosions, spreads poisons, or uses other dangerous means that lead to people's serious injuries or death or cause public or private property to suffer major losses is to be sentenced to not less than ten years of fixed-term imprisonment, life imprisonment or death.

Whoever commits the crimes in the preceding paragraph negligently is to be sentenced to not more than seven years of fixed-term imprisonment or criminal detention.

Article 107 Whoever sabotages trains, motor vehicles, streetcars, ships or airplanes in a manner sufficient to threaten the overturning or destruction of such trains, motor vehicles, streetcars, ships or airplanes, in cases where serious consequences have not been caused, is to be sentenced to not less than three years and not more than ten years of fixed-term imprisonment.

Article 108 Whoever sabotages railroads, bridges, tunnels, highways, airports, waterways, lighthouses or signs, or conducts other destructive activities in a manner sufficient to threaten the overturning or destruction of trains, motor vehicles, streetcars, ships or airplanes, in cases where serious consequences have not been caused, is to be sentenced to not less than three years and not more than ten years of fixed-term imprisonment.

Article 109 Whoever sabotages electric power, gas or other combustible or explosive equipment, endangering public security, in cases where serious consequences have not been caused, is to be sentenced to not less than three years and not more than ten years of fixed-term imprisonment.

Article 110 Whoever sabotages means of transportation, transportation equipment, electric power or gas equipment, or combustible or explosive equipment, causing serious consequences, is to be sentenced to not less than ten years of fixed-term imprisonment, life imprisonment or death.

Whoever commits the crime in the preceding paragraph negligently is to be sentenced to not more than seven years of fixed-term imprisonment or criminal detention.

Article 111 Whoever sabotages broadcasting stations, telegraph, telephone or other communications equipment, harming public security, is to be sentenced to not more than seven years of fixed-term imprisonment or criminal detention; in cases where serious consequences have been caused, the sentence is to be not less than seven years of fixed-term imprisonment.

Whoever commits the crime in the preceding paragraph negligently is to be sentenced to not more than seven years of fixed-term imprisonment or criminal detention.

Article 112†† Whoever illegally manufactures, trades in or transports guns or ammunition, or steals or seizes the guns or ammunition of state organs, military or police personnel or people's militia, is to be sentenced to not more than seven years of fixed-term imprisonment; when the circumstances are serious, the sentence is to be not less than seven years of fixed-term imprisonment or life imprisonment.

Article 113 Communications or transportation personnel who violate the rules, thereby giving rise to major accidents leading to people's serious injury or death or causing public or private property to suffer major losses, is to be sentenced to not more than three years of fixed-term imprisonment or criminal detention; when the circumstances are especially odious, the sentence is to be not less than three years and not more than seven years of fixed-term imprisonment.

Persons who are not communications or transportation personnel and who commit the crime in the preceding paragraph are to be punished in accordance with the stipulations of the preceding paragraph.

Article 114 The staff and workers of factories, mines, forestry centres, construction enterprises or other enterprises and institutions who do not submit to management and violate the rules or force workers to work in a risky way in violation of the rules, thereby giving rise to major accidents involving injury or death and causing serious consequences, are to be sentenced to not more than three years of fixed-term imprisonment or criminal detention; when the circumstances are especially odious, the sentence is to be not less than three years and not more than seven years of fixed-term imprisonment.

Article 115 Whoever violates the regulations on the control of articles of an explosive, combustible, radioactive, poisonous or corrosive nature, giving rise to a major accident in the course of production, storage, transportation or use and causing serious consequences, is to be sentenced to not more than three years of fixed-term imprisonment or criminal detention; when the consequences are especially serious, the sentence is to be not less than three years and not more than seven years of fixed-term imprisonment.

CHAPTER III CRIMES OF UNDERMINING THE SOCIALIST ECONOMIC ORDER

Article 116 Whoever violates the Customs laws and regulations, engaging in smuggling, if the circumstances are serious, in addition to having the smuggled articles confiscated and a fine possibly imposed in accordance with the Customs laws and regulations, is to be sentenced to not more than three years of fixed-term imprisonment or criminal detention, and may in addition be sentenced to confiscation of property.

Article 117 Whoever violates the laws and regulations on the control of monetary affairs, foreign exchange, gold and silver, or industrial and commercial affairs, engaging in speculation, if the circumstances are serious, is to be sentenced to not more than three years of fixed-term imprisonment or criminal detention, and may in addition or exclusively be sentenced to a fine or confiscation of property.

Article 118† Whoever makes a regular occupation of smuggling or speculation, or smuggles or speculates in huge amounts, or is ringleader of a group that smuggles or speculates, is to be sentenced to not less than three years and not more than ten years of fixed-term imprisonment, and may in addition be sentenced to confiscation of property.

Article 119 State personnel who take advantage of their office to commit the crime of smuggling or speculation are to be given a heavier punishment.

Article 120 Whoever, for the purpose of reaping profits, counterfeits or resells planned supply cou-

---

† Articles where this symbol appears have been revised by the Decision of the Standing Committee of the National People's Congress Regarding the Severe Punishment of Criminals Who Seriously Undermine the Economy. *See* pp. 229-33 below. — *Trans.*

pons is, if the circumstances are serious, to be sentenced to not more than three years of fixed-term imprisonment or criminal detention, and may in addition or exclusively be sentenced to a fine or confiscation of property.

In the case of a ringleader in committing the crime in the preceding paragraph or especially serious circumstances, the sentence is to be not less than three years and not more than seven years of fixed-term imprisonment, and the offender may in addition be sentenced to confiscation of property.

Article 121 Those directly responsible for violating tax laws and regulations, evading taxes or resisting taxes, if the circumstances are serious, in addition to making up the tax due and paying any fine possibly imposed in accordance with the tax laws and regulations, are to be sentenced to not more than three years of fixed-term imprisonment or criminal detention.

Article 122 Whoever counterfeits national currency or traffics in counterfeited national currency is to be sentenced to not less than three years and not more than seven years of fixed-term imprisonment, and may in addition be sentenced to a fine or confiscation of property.

In the case of a ringleader in committing the crime in the preceding paragraph or especially serious circumstances, the sentence is to be not less than seven years of fixed-term imprisonment or life imprisonment, and the offender may in addition be sentenced to confiscation of property.

Article 123 Whoever counterfeits checks, share certificates or other valuable securities is to be sentenced to not more than seven years of fixed-term imprisonment, and may in addition be sentenced to a fine.

Article 124 Whoever, for the purpose of reaping profits, counterfeits tickets for vehicles or ships, postage stamps, tax stamps or invoices is to be sentenced to not more than two years of fixed-term imprisonment, criminal detention or a fine; when the circumstances are serious, the sentence is to be not less than two years and not more than seven years of fixed-term imprisonment, and the offender may in addition be sentenced to a fine.

Article 125 Whoever, in order to give vent to spite, to retaliate, or for other personal motives, destroys machinery or equipment, cruelly injures or slaughters draft animals, or uses other means to sabotage collective production is to be sentenced to not more than two years of fixed-term imprisonment or criminal detention; when the circumstances are serious, the sentence is to be not less than two years and not more than seven years of fixed-term imprisonment.

Article 126 Those directly responsible for misappropriating state funds and materials allocated for disaster relief, emergencies, flood prevention and control, for disabled servicemen and the families of revolutionary martyrs and servicemen, and social relief, when the circumstances are serious, causing the interests of the state and the masses of people to suffer major damage, are to be sentenced to not more than three years of fixed-term imprisonment or criminal detention; when the circumstances are especially serious, the sentence is to be not less than three years and not more than seven years of fixed-term imprisonment.

Article 127 Where, in violation of the laws and regulations on trademark control, an industrial or commercial enterprise falsely passes off trademarks already registered by another enterprise, the persons directly responsible are to be sentenced to not more than three years of fixed-term imprisonment, criminal detention or a fine.

Article 128 Whoever violates the laws and regulations on forestry protection, illegally chopping down trees or denuding forests or other woods, when the circumstances are serious, is to be sentenced to not more than three years of fixed-term imprisonment or criminal detention, and may in addition or exclusively be sentenced to a fine.

Article 129 Whoever violates the laws and regulations on the protection of aquatic resources, catching aquatic products in an area where fishing is prohibited or during a period when fishing is prohibited, or using prohibited implements or methods to catch aquatic products, when the circumstances are serious, is to be sentenced to not more than two years of fixed-term imprisonment, criminal detention or a fine.

Article 130 Whoever violates the hunting laws and regulations, hunting in an area where hunting is prohibited or during a period when hunting is prohibited, or using prohibited implements or methods for hunting, damaging rare birds, beasts or other wild animal resources, when the circumstances are serious, is to be sentenced to not more than two years of fixed-term imprisonment, criminal detention or a fine.

CHAPTER IV CRIMES OF INFRINGING UPON THE RIGHTS OF THE PERSON AND THE DEMOCRATIC RIGHTS OF CITIZENS

Article 131 The rights of the person, the democratic rights and the other rights of citizens are to be protected and are not to be unlawfully infringed by any person or any organ. When the circumstances of unlawful infringement are serious, those directly responsible are to be given criminal sanctions.

Article 132 Whoever intentionally kills another is to be sentenced to death, life imprisonment or not less than ten years of fixed-term imprisonment; when the circumstances are relatively minor, he is to be sentenced to not less than three years and not more than ten years of fixed-term imprisonment.

Article 133 Whoever negligently kills another is to be sentenced to not more than five years of fixed-term imprisonment; when the circumstances are especially odious, the sentence is to be not less than five years of fixed-term imprisonment. Where this Law has other stipulations, matters are to be handled in accordance with such stipulations.

Article 134†† Whoever intentionally injures the person of another is to be sentenced to not more than three years of fixed-term imprisonment or criminal detention.

Whoever commits the crime in the preceding paragraph and causes a person's serious injury is to be sentenced to not less than three years and not more than seven years of fixed-term imprisonment; if he causes a person's death, he is to be sentenced to not less than seven years of fixed-term imprisonment. Where this Law has other stipulations, matters are to be handled in accordance with such stipulations.

Article 135 Whoever negligently injures another and causes him serious injury is to be sentenced to not more than two years of fixed-term imprisonment or criminal detention; when the circumstances are especially odious, the sentence is to be not less than two years and not more than seven years of fixed-term imprisonment. Where this Law has other stipulations, matters are to be handled in accordance with such stipulations.

Article 136 The use of torture to coerce a statement is strictly prohibited. State personnel who inflict torture on an offender to coerce a statement are to be sentenced to not more than three years of fixed-term imprisonment or criminal detention. Whoever causes a person's injury or disability through corporal punishment is to be handled under the crime of injury and given a heavier punishment.

Article 137 Assembling a crowd for "beating, smashing and looting" is strictly prohibited. Whoever causes a person's injury, disability or death through "beating, smashing and looting" is to be handled under the crime of injury or the crime of killing another. In cases where articles of public or private property are destroyed or forcibly taken and carried away, in addition to the ordering of restitution or compensation, ringleaders are to be handled under the crime of robbery.

Whoever commits the crime in the preceding paragraph may be sentenced exclusively to deprivation of political rights.

Article 138 Using any method or means falsely to accuse and frame cadres or the masses is strictly prohibited. Anyone who fabricates facts to accuse falsely and frame another person (including a criminal) is to be given a criminal sanction by reference to the nature, circumstances, consequences and sentencing standards of the crime of which he falsely accuses another person and frames him. State personnel who commit the crime of falsely accusing and framing others are to be given a heavier punishment.

When it is not a case of intentional false accusation and framing but rather a case of a mistaken complaint or an accusation at variance with the facts, the stipulations of the preceding paragraph do not apply.

Article 139 Whoever by violence, coercion or other means rapes a woman is to be sentenced to not less than three years and not more than ten years of fixed-term imprisonment.

Whoever has sexual relations with a girl under the age of fourteen is to be deemed to have committed rape and is to be given a heavier punishment.

Whoever commits a crime in the preceding two paragraphs, when the circumstances are especially serious or a person's injury or death is caused, is to be sentenced to not less than ten years of fixed-term imprisonment, life imprisonment or death.

When two or more persons jointly commit rape in

succession, they are to be given a heavier punishment.

Article 140†† Whoever forces women into prostitution is to be sentenced to not less than three years and not more than ten years of fixed-term imprisonment.

Article 141†† Whoever abducts and sells people is to be sentenced to not more than five years of fixed-term imprisonment; when the circumstances are serious, the sentence is to be not less than five years of fixed-term imprisonment.

Article 142 Whoever violates the stipulations of the election laws and by violence, threat, deception, bribery or other unlawful means sabotages elections or obstructs the electorate in its free exercise of the right to elect and to be elected is to be sentenced to not more than three years of fixed-term imprisonment or criminal detention.

Article 143 The unlawful detention of another person or the unlawful deprivation of his freedom of the person by any other means is strictly prohibited. A violator is to be sentenced to not more than three years of fixed-term imprisonment, criminal detention or deprivation of political rights. In circumstances where beating or humiliation is involved, a heavier punishment is to be given.

Whoever commits the crime in the preceding paragraph and causes a person's serious injury is to be sentenced to not less than three years and not more than ten years of fixed-term imprisonment; when he causes a person's death, he is to be sentenced to not less than seven years of fixed-term imprisonment.

Article 144 Whoever unlawfully subjects another

person to control, unlawfully searches another's person or residence, or unlawfully intrudes into another's residence is to be sentenced to not more than three years of fixed-term imprisonment or criminal detention.

Article 145 Whoever, by violence or other methods including the use of "big character posters" and "small character posters", publicly insults another person or trumps up facts to defame another person, when the circumstances are serious, is to be sentenced to not more than three years of fixed-term imprisonment, criminal detention or deprivation of political rights.

The crime in the preceding paragraph is to be handled only upon complaint. However, cases of serious harm to the social order and to the interests of the state are exceptions.

Article 146 State personnel who abuse their powers and use public office for private gain, carrying out retaliation or frame-ups against complainants, petitioners or critics, are to be sentenced to not more than two years of fixed-term imprisonment or criminal detention; when the circumstances are serious, the sentence is to be not less than two years and not more than seven years of fixed-term imprisonment.

Article 147 State personnel who unlawfully deprive citizens of their legitimate freedom of religious belief and infringe upon the customs and habits of minority ethnic groups, when the circumstances are serious, are to be sentenced to not more than two years of fixed-term imprisonment or criminal detention.

Article 148 During investigation or adjudication, a witness, expert witness, recorder or interpreter who, with respect to circumstances bearing an important relation to the case, intentionally gives false proof or makes a false expert evaluation, record or translation, with the intention of framing another person or concealing criminal evidence, is to be sentenced to not more than two years of fixed-term imprisonment or criminal detention; when the circumstances are serious, the sentence is to be not less than two years and not more than seven years of fixed-term imprisonment.

Article 149 Whoever conceals, destroys or unlawfully opens the letters of another person, infringing upon a citizen's right to freedom of correspondence, when the circumstances are serious, is to be sentenced to not more than one year of fixed-term imprisonment or criminal detention.

CHAPTER V   CRIMES OF PROPERTY VIOLATION

Article 150 Whoever, by violence, coercion or other methods, steals articles of public or private property is to be sentenced to not less than three years and not more than ten years of fixed-term imprisonment.

Whoever commits the crime in the preceding paragraph, when the circumstances are serious or a person's serious injury or death is caused, is to be sentenced to not less than ten years of fixed-term imprisonment, life imprisonment or death, and may in addition be sentenced to confiscation of property.

Article 151 Whoever steals, swindles or forcibly seizes articles of public or private property of a relatively large amount is to be sentenced to not more than five years of fixed-term imprisonment, criminal detention or control.

Article 152† Whoever habitually steals or habitually swindles, or steals, swindles or forcibly seizes articles of public or private property of a huge amount is to be sentenced to not less than five years and not more than ten years of fixed-term imprisonment; when the circumstances are especially serious, the sentence is to be not less than ten years of fixed-term imprisonment or life imprisonment, and the offender may in addition be sentenced to confiscation of property.

Article 153 Whoever commits the crimes of theft, fraud or forcible seizure and, at the scene, uses violence or threats by the appearance of violence in order to conceal booty, resist arrest or destroy criminal evidence, is to be punished in accordance with Article 150 of this Law on the crime of robbery.

Article 154 Whoever extorts articles of public or private property by blackmail is to be sentenced to not more than three years of fixed-term imprisonment or criminal detention; when the circumstances are serious, the sentence is to be not less than three years and not more than seven years of fixed-term imprisonment.

Article 155 State personnel who take advantage of their office to engage in corruption involving articles of public property are to be sentenced to not more than five years of fixed-term imprisonment or criminal detention; if the amount involved is huge and the circumstances are serious, the sentence is to be not less than five years of fixed-term imprisonment; if the circumstances are especially serious, the sentence is to be life imprisonment or death.

A person who commits the crime in the preceding paragraph is to be sentenced in addition to confiscation of property or ordered to make restitution or pay compensation.

Personnel entrusted by state organs, enterprises, institutions or people's organizations to engage in public service who commit the crime in the first paragraph are to be punished in accordance with the stipulations of the two preceding paragraphs.

Article 156 Whoever intentionally destroys articles of public or private property, when the circumstances are serious, is to be sentenced to not more than three years of fixed-term imprisonment, criminal detention or a fine.

CHAPTER VI CRIMES OF DISRUPTING THE ORDER OF SOCIAL ADMINISTRATION

Article 157 Whoever, by violent or threatening methods, obstructs state personnel from carrying out their functions according to law, or refuses to carry out judgments or orders of people's courts that already have become legally effective, is to be sentenced to not more than three years of fixed-term imprisonment, criminal detention, a fine or deprivation of political rights.

Article 158 The use by any person of any means to disturb the social order is prohibited. When the circumstances of disturbance of the social order are serious, so that work, production, business and education or scientific research cannot be conducted and the state and society suffer serious losses, ringleaders are to be sentenced to not more than five years of fixed-term imprisonment, criminal detention, control or deprivation of political rights.

Article 159 In cases of assembling a crowd to disturb order at stations, wharves, civil aviation stations, market places, public parks, theatres, exhibitions, sports grounds or other public places, or assembling a crowd to block traffic or undermine traffic order, or resist or obstruct state security administration personnel who are carrying out their functions according to law, when the circumstances are serious, ringleaders are to be sentenced to not more than five years of fixed-term imprisonment, criminal detention, control or deprivation of political rights.

Article 160† Whoever assembles a crowd to have brawls, stir up fights and cause trouble, humiliate women, or engage in other hooligan activities, undermining public order, when the circumstances are odious, is to be sentenced to not more than seven years of fixed-term imprisonment, criminal detention or control.

Ringleaders of hooligan groups are to be sentenced to not less than seven years of fixed-term imprisonment.

Article 161 A criminal element who has been arrested or is in custody according to law and escapes, in addition to receiving a sentence for the crime he originally committed or serving the term to which he was originally sentenced, is to receive an increase in sentence of not more than five years of fixed-term imprisonment or criminal detention.

Whoever commits the crime in the preceding paragraph by violent or threatening methods is to be sentenced to not less than two years and not more than seven years of fixed-term imprisonment.

Article 162 Whoever harbours counterrevolutionary elements or gives false proof to protect them is to be sentenced to not more than three years of fixed-term imprisonment, criminal detention or control; when the circumstances are serious, the sentence is to be not less than three years and not more than ten years of fixed-term imprisonment.

Whoever harbours other criminal elements or gives false proof to protect them is to be sentenced to not more than two years of fixed-term imprisonment, criminal detention or control; when the circumstances are serious, the sentence is to be not less than two years and not more than seven years of fixed-term imprisonment.

Persons who commit a crime in the two preceding paragraphs and who conspire in advance are to be deemed to have committed a joint crime.

Article 163 Whoever violates gun control regulations, privately storing guns or ammunition and refusing to hand them over, is to be sentenced to not more than two years of fixed-term imprisonment or criminal detention.

Article 164 Whoever, for the purpose of reaping profits, manufactures or sells bogus medicines, harming the people's health, is to be sentenced to not more than two years of fixed-term imprisonment, criminal detention or control, and may in addition or exclusively be sentenced to a fine; when serious consequences have been caused, the sentence is to be not less than two years and not more than seven years of fixed-term imprisonment, and the offender may in addition be sentenced to a fine.

Article 165 Sorcerers or witches who use superstition to engage in the activities of rumour-mongering or swindling articles of property are to be sentenced to not more than two years of fixed-term imprisonment, criminal detention or control; when the circumstances are serious, the sentence is to be not less than two years and not more than seven years of fixed-term imprisonment.

Article 166 Whoever poses as state personnel to cheat and bluff is to be sentenced to not more than three years of fixed-term imprisonment, criminal detention, control or deprivation of political rights; when the circumstances are serious, the sentence is to be not less than three years and not more than ten years of fixed-term imprisonment.

Article 167 Whoever forges, alters or steals, forcibly seizes or destroys official documents, certificates or seals of state organs, enterprises, institutions or people's organizations is to be sentenced to not more than three years of fixed-term imprisonment, criminal detention, control or deprivation of political rights; when the circumstances are serious, the sentence is to be not less than three years and not more than ten years of fixed-term imprisonment.

Article 168 Whoever, for the purpose of reaping profits, assembles a crowd to engage in gambling or makes an occupation of gambling is to be sentenced to not more than three years of fixed-term imprisonment, criminal detention or control, and may in addition be sentenced to a fine.

Article 169†† Whoever, for the purpose of reaping profits, lures women into prostitution or shelters them in prostitution, is to be sentenced to not more than five years of fixed-term imprisonment, criminal detention or control; when the circumstances are serious, the sentence is to be not less than five years of fixed-term imprisonment, and the offender may in addition be sentenced to a fine or confiscation of property.

Article 170† Whoever, for the purpose of reaping profits, produces or sells pornographic books or pictures is to be sentenced to not more than three years of fixed-term imprisonment, criminal detention or control, and may in addition be sentenced to a fine.

Article 171† Whoever manufactures, sells or transports opium, heroin, morphine or other narcotics is to be sentenced to not more than five years of fixed-term imprisonment or criminal detention, and may in addition be sentenced to a fine.

Whoever persistently or in large amounts manufactures, sells or transports the narcotics in the preceding paragraph is to be sentenced to not less than five years of fixed-term imprisonment, and may in addition be sentenced to confiscation of property.

Article 172 Whoever conceals goods that he clearly knows to be stolen, obtained through crime, or acts as agent for the sale of them is to be sentenced to not more than three years of fixed-term imprisonment, criminal detention or control, and may in addition or exclusively be sentenced to a fine.

Article 173† Whoever violates the laws and regulations on protection of cultural relics, stealing and exporting precious cultural relics, is to be sentenced to not less than three years and not more than ten years of fixed-term imprisonment, and may in addition be sentenced to a fine; when the circumstances are serious, the sentence is to be not less than ten years of fixed-term imprisonment or life imprisonment, and the offender may in addition be sentenced to confiscation of property.

Article 174 Whoever intentionally sabotages precious cultural relics or places of historic interest or scenic beauty protected by the state is to be sentenced to not more than seven years of fixed-term imprisonment or criminal detention.

Article 175 Whoever intentionally sabotages boundary tablets, boundary markers or survey indicators of a permanent nature along the borders of the country is to be sentenced to not more than three years of fixed-term imprisonment or criminal detention.

Where it is for the purpose of treason, punishment is to be in accordance with that for crimes of counterrevolution.

Article 176 Whoever violates the laws and regulations that control leaving and entering the country, secretly crossing the national boundary (or borderline), when the circumstances are serious, is to be sentenced to not more than one year of fixed-term imprisonment, criminal detention or control.

Article 177 Whoever, for the purpose of reaping profits, organizes or transports other persons secretly to cross the national boundary (or borderline) is to be sentenced to not more than five years of fixed-term imprisonment, criminal detention or control, and may in addition be sentenced to a fine.

Article 178 Whoever violates national border health and quarantine regulations, causing the spread of quarantined contagious diseases or causing a serious danger of the spread of quarantined contagious diseases, is to be sentenced to not more than three years of fixed-term imprisonment or criminal detention, and may in addition or exclusively be sentenced to a fine.

CHAPTER VII CRIMES OF DISRUPTING MARRIAGE AND THE FAMILY

Article 179 Whoever uses violence to interfere with the freedom of marriage of others is to be sentenced to not more than two years of fixed-term imprisonment or criminal detention.

Whoever commits the crime in the preceding paragraph and causes the death of the victim is to be sentenced to not less than two years and not more than seven years of fixed-term imprisonment.

The crime in the first paragraph is to be handled only upon complaint.

Article 180 Whoever has a spouse and commits bigamy or whoever marries another person, clearly knowing that the other has a spouse, is to be sentenced to not more than two years of fixed-term imprisonment or criminal detention.

Article 181 Whoever cohabits with or marries someone, clearly knowing the person to be the spouse of a member of the armed forces in active service, is to be sentenced to not more than three years of fixed-term imprisonment.

Article 182 Whoever abuses a member of his family, when the circumstances are odious, is to be sentenced to not more than two years of fixed-term imprisonment, criminal detention or control.

Whoever commits the crime in the preceding paragraph and causes serious injury or death to the victim is to be sentenced to not less than two years and not more than seven years of fixed-term imprisonment.

The crime in the first paragraph is to be handled only upon complaint.

Article 183 Whoever has a duty to support aged persons, children, sick persons or others lacking the ability to live independently, but refuses to provide such support, when the circumstances are odious, is to be sentenced to not more than five years of fixed-term imprisonment, criminal detention or control.

Article 184 Whoever abducts a boy or girl under the age of fourteen, cutting the child off from his family or guardian, is to be sentenced to not more than five years of fixed-term imprisonment or criminal detention.

CHAPTER VIII CRIMES OF DERELICTION OF DUTY

Article 185† State personnel who take advantage of their office to accept bribes are to be sentenced to not more than five years of fixed-term imprisonment or criminal detention. The funds or articles received as bribes are to be confiscated, and public funds or articles recovered.

Whoever commits the crime in the preceding paragraph and causes the interests of the state or citizens to suffer serious losses is to be sentenced to not less than five years of fixed-term imprisonment.

Whoever offers or introduces a bribe to state personnel is to be sentenced to not more than three years of fixed-term imprisonment or criminal detention.

Article 186 State personnel who violate the laws and regulations of the state on protection of secrets, disclosing important state secrets, when the circumstances are serious, are to be sentenced to not more than seven years of fixed-term imprisonment, criminal detention or deprivation of political rights.

Where persons who are not state personnel commit the crime in the preceding paragraph, consideration is to be given according to the circumstances to punishing them in accordance with the stipulations of the preceding paragraph.

Article 187 State personnel who, because of neglect of duty, cause public property or the interests of the state and the people to suffer major losses are to be sentenced to not more than five years of fixed-term imprisonment or criminal detention.

Article 188 Judicial personnel who engage in

self-seeking misconduct, subjecting to prosecution persons they clearly know to be innocent or intentionally protecting from prosecution persons they clearly know to be guilty, or, intentionally confounding right and wrong, rendering orders and judgments that misuse the law, are to be sentenced to not more than five years of fixed-term imprisonment, criminal detention or deprivation of political rights; when the circumstances are especially serious, the sentence is to be not less than five years of fixed-term imprisonment.

Article 189 Judicial personnel who violate laws and regulations on prison management, subjecting imprisoned persons to corporal punishment and abuse, when the circumstances are serious, are to be sentenced to not more than three years of fixed-term imprisonment or criminal detention; when the circumstances are especially serious, the sentence is to be not less than three years and not more than ten years of fixed-term imprisonment.

Article 190 Judicial personnel who release criminals of their own accord are to be sentenced to not more than five years of fixed-term imprisonment or criminal detention; when the circumstances are serious, the sentence is to be not less than five years and not more than ten years of fixed-term imprisonment.

Article 191 Postal and telecommunications personnel who open, conceal or destroy mail or telegrams of their own accord are to be sentenced to not more than two years of fixed-term imprisonment or criminal detention.

Whoever steals articles of property in the course of

committing the crime in the preceding paragraph is to be given a heavier punishment under Article 155 on the crime of corruption.

Article 192 For state personnel who commit a crime in this Chapter, if the circumstances are minor, the department in charge may give consideration according to the circumstances to giving them administrative sanctions.

中华人民共和国刑法

(一九七九年七月一日第五届全国人民代表大会第二次会议通过,自一九八〇年一月一日起施行)

目 录

第一编 总 则 ·· 69
  第一章 刑法的指导思想、任务和适用范围 ····· 69
  第二章 犯罪 ·· 71
    第一节 犯罪和刑事责任 ································ 71
    第二节 犯罪的预备、未遂和中止 ·················· 74
    第三节 共同犯罪 ·· 74
  第三章 刑罚 ·· 75
    第一节 刑罚的种类 ······································· 75
    第二节 管制 ·· 76
    第三节 拘役 ·· 77
    第四节 有期徒刑、无期徒刑 ·························· 78
    第五节 死刑 ·· 78
    第六节 罚金 ·· 79
    第七节 剥夺政治权利 ··································· 79
    第八节 没收财产 ·· 80
  第四章 刑罚的具体运用 ····································· 81
    第一节 量刑 ·· 81
    第二节 累犯 ·· 82
    第三节 自首 ·· 82
    第四节 数罪并罚 ·· 82
    第五节 缓刑 ·· 83
    第六节 减刑 ·· 84
    第七节 假释 ·· 84
    第八节 时效 ·· 85
  第五章 其他规定 ·· 86

67

第二编 分　　则 …………………………………………………89
　第一章　反革命罪 ……………………………………………89
　第二章　危害公共安全罪 ……………………………………92
　第三章　破坏社会主义经济秩序罪 …………………………95
　第四章　侵犯公民人身权利、民主权利罪 …………………97
　第五章　侵犯财产罪 …………………………………………101
　第六章　妨害社会管理秩序罪 ………………………………103
　第七章　妨害婚姻、家庭罪 …………………………………107
　第八章　渎职罪 ………………………………………………108

第一编 总 则

第一章 刑法的指导思想、任务和适用范围

第一条 中华人民共和国刑法，以马克思列宁主义毛泽东思想为指针，以宪法为根据，依照惩办与宽大相结合的政策，结合我国各族人民实行无产阶级领导的、工农联盟为基础的人民民主专政即无产阶级专政和进行社会主义革命、社会主义建设的具体经验及实际情况制定。

第二条 中华人民共和国刑法的任务，是用刑罚同一切反革命和其他刑事犯罪行为作斗争，以保卫无产阶级专政制度，保护社会主义的全民所有的财产和劳动群众集体所有的财产，保护公民私人所有的合法财产，保护公民的人身权利、民主权利和其他权利，维护社会秩序、生产秩序、工作秩序、教学科研秩序和人民群众生活秩序，保障社会主义革命和社会主义建设事业的顺利进行。

第三条 凡在中华人民共和国领域内犯罪

的,除法律有特别规定的以外,都适用本法。

凡在中华人民共和国船舶或者飞机内犯罪的,也适用本法。

犯罪的行为或者结果有一项发生在中华人民共和国领域内的,就认为是在中华人民共和国领域内犯罪。

第四条 中华人民共和国公民在中华人民共和国领域外犯下列各罪的,适用本法:

(一)反革命罪;

(二)伪造国家货币罪(第一百二十二条),伪造有价证券罪(第一百二十三条);

(三)贪污罪(第一百五十五条),受贿罪(第一百八十五条),泄露国家机密罪(第一百八十六条);

(四)冒充国家工作人员招摇撞骗罪(第一百六十六条),伪造公文、证件、印章罪(第一百六十七条)。

第五条 中华人民共和国公民在中华人民共和国领域外犯前条以外的罪,而按本法规定的最低刑为三年以上有期徒刑的,也适用本法;但是按照犯罪地的法律不受处罚的除外。

第六条 外国人在中华人民共和国领域外对中华人民共和国国家或者公民犯罪,而按本法规定的最低刑为三年以上有期徒刑的,可以适用本法；但是按照犯罪地的法律不受处罚的除外。

第七条 凡在中华人民共和国领域外犯罪、依照本法应当负刑事责任的，虽然经过外国审判，仍然可以依照本法处理；但是在外国已经受过刑罚处罚的，可以免除或者减轻处罚。

第八条 享有外交特权和豁免权的外国人的刑事责任问题，通过外交途径解决。

第九条 本法自一九八〇年一月一日起生效。中华人民共和国成立以后本法施行以前的行为，如果当时的法律、法令、政策不认为是犯罪的，适用当时的法律、法令、政策。如果当时的法律、法令、政策认为是犯罪的，依照本法总则第四章第八节的规定应当追诉的，按照当时的法律、法令、政策追究刑事责任。但是，如果本法不认为是犯罪或者处刑较轻的，适用本法。

第二章 犯 罪

第一节 犯罪和刑事责任

第十条 一切危害国家主权和领土完整，危害无产阶级专政制度，破坏社会主义革命和社会主义建设，破坏社会秩序，侵犯全民所有的财产或者劳动群众集体所有的财产，侵犯公民私人所有的合法财产，侵犯公民的人身权利、民主权利和其他权利,以及其他危害社会的行为,依照法律应当受刑罚处罚的,都是犯罪;但是情节显著轻微危害不大的,不认为是犯罪。

第十一条 明知自己的行为会发生危害社会的结果,并且希望或者放任这种结果发生,因而构成犯罪的,是故意犯罪。

故意犯罪,应当负刑事责任。

第十二条 应当预见自己的行为可能发生危害社会的结果,因为疏忽大意而没有预见,或者已经预见而轻信能够避免,以致发生这种结果的,是过失犯罪。

过失犯罪,法律有规定的才负刑事责任。

第十三条 行为在客观上虽然造成了损害结果,但是不是出于故意或者过失,而是由于不能抗拒或者不能预见的原因所引起的,不认为是犯罪。

第十四条 已满十六岁的人犯罪,应当负刑事责任。

已满十四岁不满十六岁的人,犯杀人、重伤、抢劫、放火、惯窃罪或者其他严重破坏社会秩序罪,应当负刑事责任。

已满十四岁不满十八岁的人犯罪,应当从轻或者减轻处罚。

因不满十六岁不处罚的,责令他的家长或者

监护人加以管教；在必要的时候，也可以由政府收容教养。

第十五条 精神病人在不能辨认或者不能控制自己行为的时候造成危害结果的，不负刑事责任；但是应当责令他的家属或者监护人严加看管和医疗。

间歇性的精神病人在精神正常的时候犯罪，应当负刑事责任。

醉酒的人犯罪，应当负刑事责任。

第十六条 又聋又哑的人或者盲人犯罪，可以从轻、减轻或者免除处罚。

第十七条 为了使公共利益、本人或者他人的人身和其他权利免受正在进行的不法侵害，而采取的正当防卫行为，不负刑事责任。

正当防卫超过必要限度造成不应有的危害的，应当负刑事责任；但是应当酌情减轻或者免除处罚。

第十八条 为了使公共利益、本人或者他人的人身和其他权利免受正在发生的危险，不得已采取的紧急避险行为，不负刑事责任。

紧急避险超过必要限度造成不应有的危害的，应当负刑事责任；但是应当酌情减轻或者免除处罚。

第一款中关于避免本人危险的规定，不适用

于职务上、业务上负有特定责任的人。

第二节 犯罪的预备、未遂和中止

第十九条 为了犯罪,准备工具、制造条件的,是犯罪预备。

对于预备犯,可以比照既遂犯从轻、减轻处罚或者免除处罚。

第二十条 已经着手实行犯罪,由于犯罪分子意志以外的原因而未得逞的,是犯罪未遂。

对于未遂犯,可以比照既遂犯从轻或者减轻处罚。

第二十一条 在犯罪过程中,自动中止犯罪或者自动有效地防止犯罪结果发生的,是犯罪中止。

对于中止犯,应当免除或者减轻处罚。

第三节 共同犯罪

第二十二条 共同犯罪是指二人以上共同故意犯罪。

二人以上共同过失犯罪,不以共同犯罪论处;应当负刑事责任的,按照他们所犯的罪分别处罚。

第二十三条 组织、领导犯罪集团进行犯罪

活动的或者在共同犯罪中起主要作用的,是主犯。

对于主犯,除本法分则已有规定的以外,应当从重处罚。

第二十四条 在共同犯罪中起次要或者辅助作用的,是从犯。

对于从犯,应当比照主犯从轻、减轻处罚或者免除处罚。

第二十五条 对于被胁迫、被诱骗参加犯罪的,应当按照他的犯罪情节,比照从犯减轻处罚或者免除处罚。

第二十六条 教唆他人犯罪的,应当按照他在共同犯罪中所起的作用处罚。教唆不满十八岁的人犯罪的,应当从重处罚。

如果被教唆的人没有犯被教唆的罪,对于教唆犯,可以从轻或者减轻处罚。

第三章 刑 罚

第一节 刑罚的种类

第二十七条 刑罚分为主刑和附加刑。

第二十八条 主刑的种类如下:

(一)管制;

(二)拘役;

（三）有期徒刑；

（四）无期徒刑；

（五）死刑。

第二十九条 附加刑的种类如下：

（一）罚金；

（二）剥夺政治权利；

（三）没收财产。

附加刑也可以独立适用。

第三十条 对于犯罪的外国人，可以独立适用或者附加适用驱逐出境。

第三十一条 由于犯罪行为而使被害人遭受经济损失的，对犯罪分子除依法给予刑事处分外，并应根据情况判处赔偿经济损失。

第三十二条 对于犯罪情节轻微不需要判处刑罚的，可以免予刑事处分，但可以根据案件的不同情况，予以训诫或者责令具结悔过、赔礼道歉、赔偿损失，或者由主管部门予以行政处分。

第二节 管　　制

第三十三条 管制的期限，为三个月以上二年以下。

管制由人民法院判决，由公安机关执行。

第三十四条 被判处管制的犯罪分子，在执行期间，必须遵守下列规定：

（一）遵守法律、法令，服从群众监督，积极参加集体劳动生产或者工作；

（二）向执行机关定期报告自己的活动情况；

（三）迁居或者外出必须报经执行机关批准。

对于被判处管制的犯罪分子，在劳动中应当同工同酬。

第三十五条 被判处管制的犯罪分子，管制期满，执行机关应即向本人和有关的群众宣布解除管制。

第三十六条 管制的刑期，从判决执行之日起计算；判决执行以前先行羁押的，羁押一日折抵刑期二日。

第三节 拘 役

第三十七条 拘役的期限，为十五日以上六个月以下。

第三十八条 被判处拘役的犯罪分子，由公安机关就近执行。

在执行期间，被判处拘役的犯罪分子每月可以回家一天至两天；参加劳动的，可以酌量发给报酬。

第三十九条 拘役的刑期，从判决执行之日起计算；判决以前先行羁押的，羁押一日折抵刑期一日。

第四节 有期徒刑、无期徒刑

第四十条 有期徒刑的期限，为六个月以上十五年以下。

第四十一条 被判处有期徒刑、无期徒刑的犯罪分子，在监狱或者其他劳动改造场所执行；凡有劳动能力的，实行劳动改造。

第四十二条 有期徒刑的刑期，从判决执行之日起计算；判决执行以前先行羁押的，羁押一日折抵刑期一日。

第五节 死　　刑

第四十三条 死刑只适用于罪大恶极的犯罪分子。对于应当判处死刑的犯罪分子，如果不是必须立即执行的，可以判处死刑同时宣告缓期二年执行，实行劳动改造，以观后效。

死刑除依法由最高人民法院判决的以外，都应当报请最高人民法院核准。死刑缓期执行的，可以由高级人民法院判决或者核准。

第四十四条 犯罪的时候不满十八岁的人和审判的时候怀孕的妇女，不适用死刑。已满十六岁不满十八岁的，如果所犯罪行特别严重，可以判处死刑缓期二年执行。

第四十五条 死刑用枪决的方法执行。

第四十六条 判处死刑缓期执行的，在死刑缓期执行期间，如果确有悔改，二年期满以后，减为无期徒刑；如果确有悔改并有立功表现，二年期满以后，减为十五年以上二十年以下有期徒刑；如果抗拒改造情节恶劣、查证属实的，由最高人民法院裁定或者核准，执行死刑。

第四十七条 死刑缓期执行的期间，从判决确定之日起计算。死刑缓期执行减为有期徒刑的刑期，从裁定减刑之日起计算。

第六节 罚 金

第四十八条 判处罚金，应当根据犯罪情节决定罚金数额。

第四十九条 罚金在判决指定的期限内一次或者分期缴纳。期满不缴纳的，强制缴纳。如果由于遭遇不能抗拒的灾祸缴纳确实有困难的，可以酌情减少或者免除。

第七节 剥夺政治权利

第五十条 剥夺政治权利是剥夺下列权利：

（一）选举权和被选举权；

（二）宪法第四十五条规定的各种权利；

（三）担任国家机关职务的权利；

（四）担任企业、事业单位和人民团体领导职务的权利。

第五十一条 剥夺政治权利的期限，除本法第五十三条规定外，为一年以上五年以下。

判处管制附加剥夺政治权利的，剥夺政治权利的期限与管制的期限相等，同时执行。

第五十二条 对于反革命分子应当附加剥夺政治权利；对于严重破坏社会秩序的犯罪分子，在必要的时候，也可以附加剥夺政治权利。

第五十三条 对于被判处死刑、无期徒刑的犯罪分子，应当剥夺政治权利终身。

在死刑缓期执行减为有期徒刑或者无期徒刑减为有期徒刑的时候，应当把附加剥夺政治权利的期限改为三年以上十年以下。

第五十四条 附加剥夺政治权利的刑期，从徒刑、拘役执行完毕之日或者从假释之日起计算；剥夺政治权利的效力当然施用于主刑执行期间。

第八节　没收财产

第五十五条 没收财产是没收犯罪分子个人所有财产的一部或全部。

在判处没收财产的时候，不得没收属于犯罪

分子家属所有或者应有的财产。

第五十六条 查封财产以前犯罪分子所负的正当债务，需要以没收的财产偿还的，经债权人请求，由人民法院裁定。

第四章 刑罚的具体运用

第一节 量 刑

第五十七条 对于犯罪分子决定刑罚的时候，应当根据犯罪的事实、犯罪的性质、情节和对于社会的危害程度，依照本法的有关规定判处。

第五十八条 犯罪分子具有本法规定的从重处罚、从轻处罚情节的，应当在法定刑的限度以内判处刑罚。

第五十九条 犯罪分子具有本法规定的减轻处罚情节的，应当在法定刑以下判处刑罚。

犯罪分子虽然不具有本法规定的减轻处罚情节，如果根据案件的具体情况，判处法定刑的最低刑还是过重的，经人民法院审判委员会决定，也可以在法定刑以下判处刑罚。

第六十条 犯罪分子违法所得的一切财物，应当予以追缴或者责令退赔；违禁品和供犯罪所用的本人财物，应当予以没收。

第二节 累　犯

第六十一条　被判处有期徒刑以上刑罚的犯罪分子，刑罚执行完毕或者赦免以后，在三年以内再犯应当判处有期徒刑以上刑罚之罪的，是累犯，应当从重处罚；但是过失犯罪除外。

前款规定的期限，对于被假释的犯罪分子，从假释期满之日起计算。

第六十二条　刑罚执行完毕或者赦免以后的反革命分子，在任何时候再犯反革命罪的，都以累犯论处。

第三节 自　首

第六十三条　犯罪以后自首的，可以从轻处罚。其中，犯罪较轻的，可以减轻或者免除处罚；犯罪较重的，如果有立功表现，也可以减轻或者免除处罚。

第四节 数罪并罚

第六十四条　判决宣告以前一人犯数罪的，除判处死刑和无期徒刑的以外，应当在总和刑期以下、数刑中最高刑期以上，酌情决定执行的刑期；但是管制最高不能超过三年，拘役最高不能超过一年，有期徒刑最高不能超过二十年。

如果数罪中有判处附加刑的，附加刑仍须执行。

第六十五条 判决宣告以后，刑罚还没有执行完毕以前，发现被判刑的犯罪分子在判决宣告以前还有其他罪没有判决的，应当对新发现的罪作出判决，把前后两个判决所判处的刑罚，依照本法第六十四条的规定，决定执行的刑罚。已经执行的刑期，应当计算在新判决决定的刑期以内。

第六十六条 判决宣告以后，刑罚还没有执行完毕以前，被判刑的犯罪分子又犯罪的，应当对新犯的罪作出判决，把前罪没有执行的刑罚和后罪所判处的刑罚，依照本法第六十四条的规定，决定执行的刑罚。

第五节 缓 刑

第六十七条 对于被判处拘役、三年以下有期徒刑的犯罪分子，根据犯罪分子的犯罪情节和悔罪表现，认为适用缓刑确实不致再危害社会的，可以宣告缓刑。

被宣告缓刑的犯罪分子，如果被判处附加刑，附加刑仍须执行。

第六十八条 拘役的缓刑考验期限为原判刑期以上一年以下，但是不能少于一个月。

有期徒刑的缓刑考验期限为原判刑期以上五年以下，但是不能少于一年。

缓刑考验期限，从判决确定之日起计算。

第六十九条 对于反革命犯和累犯，不适用缓刑。

第七十条 被宣告缓刑的犯罪分子，在缓刑考验期限内，由公安机关交所在单位或者基层组织予以考察，如果没有再犯新罪，缓刑考验期满，原判的刑罚就不再执行；如果再犯新罪，撤销缓刑，把前罪和后罪所判处的刑罚，依照本法第六十四条的规定，决定执行的刑罚。

第六节 减　　刑

第七十一条 被判处管制、拘役、有期徒刑、无期徒刑的犯罪分子，在执行期间，如果确有悔改或者立功表现，可以减刑。但是经过一次或者几次减刑以后实际执行的刑期，判处管制、拘役、有期徒刑的，不能少于原判刑期的二分之一；判处无期徒刑的，不能少于十年。

第七十二条 无期徒刑减为有期徒刑的刑期，从裁定减刑之日起计算。

第七节 假　　释

第七十三条 被判处有期徒刑的犯罪分子，执行原判刑期二分之一以上，被判处无期徒刑的犯罪分子，实际执行十年以上，如果确有悔改表现，不致再危害社会，可以假释。如果有特殊情节，可以不受上述执行刑期的限制。

第七十四条 有期徒刑的假释考验期限，为没有执行完毕的刑期；无期徒刑的假释考验期限，为十年。

假释考验期限，从假释之日起计算。

第七十五条 被假释的犯罪分子，在假释考验期限内，由公安机关予以监督，如果没有再犯新罪，就认为原判刑罚已经执行完毕；如果再犯新罪，撤销假释，把前罪没有执行的刑罚和后罪所判处的刑罚，依照本法第六十四条的规定，决定执行的刑罚。

第八节 时 效

第七十六条 犯罪经过下列期限不再追诉：

（一）法定最高刑为不满五年有期徒刑的，经过五年；

（二）法定最高刑为五年以上不满十年有期徒刑的，经过十年；

（三）法定最高刑为十年以上有期徒刑的，经过十五年；

（四）法定最高刑为无期徒刑、死刑的，经过二十年。如果二十年以后认为必须追诉的，须报请最高人民检察院核准。

第七十七条 在人民法院、人民检察院、公安机关采取强制措施以后,逃避侦查或者审判的,不受追诉期限的限制。

第七十八条 追诉期限从犯罪之日起计算;犯罪行为有连续或者继续状态的,从犯罪行为终了之日起计算。

在追诉期限以内又犯罪的,前罪追诉的期限从犯后罪之日起计算。

第五章 其他规定

第七十九条 本法分则没有明文规定的犯罪,可以比照本法分则最相类似的条文定罪判刑,但是应当报请最高人民法院核准。

第八十条 民族自治地方不能全部适用本法规定的,可以由自治区或者省的国家权力机关根据当地民族的政治、经济、文化的特点和本法规定的基本原则,制定变通或者补充的规定,报请全国人民代表大会常务委员会批准施行。

第八十一条 本法所说的公共财产是指下列财产:

(一)全民所有的财产;
(二)劳动群众集体所有的财产。

在国家、人民公社、合作社、合营企业和人民团体管理、使用或者运输中的私人财产，以公共财产论。

第八十二条　本法所说的公民私人所有的合法财产是指下列财产：

（一）公民的合法收入、储蓄、房屋和其他生活资料；

（二）依法归个人、家庭所有或者使用的自留地、自留畜、自留树等生产资料。

第八十三条　本法所说的国家工作人员是指一切国家机关、企业、事业单位和其他依照法律从事公务的人员。

第八十四条　本法所说的司法工作人员是指有侦讯、检察、审判、监管人犯职务的人员。

第八十五条　本法所说的重伤是指有下列情形之一的伤害：

（一）使人肢体残废或者毁人容貌的；

（二）使人丧失听觉、视觉或者其他器官机能的；

（三）其他对于人身健康有重大伤害的。

第八十六条　本法所说的首要分子是指在犯罪集团或者聚众犯罪中起组织、策划、指挥作用的犯罪分子。

第八十七条　本法所说的告诉才处理，是指

被害人告诉才处理。如果被害人因受强制、威吓无法告诉的,人民检察院和被害人的近亲属也可以告诉。

第八十八条 本法所说的以上、以下、以内,都连本数在内。

第八十九条 本法总则适用于其他有刑罚规定的法律、法令,但是其他法律有特别规定的除外。

第二编 分 则

第一章 反革命罪

第九十条 以推翻无产阶级专政的政权和社会主义制度为目的的、危害中华人民共和国的行为，都是反革命罪。

第九十一条 勾结外国，阴谋危害祖国的主权、领土完整和安全的，处无期徒刑或者十年以上有期徒刑。

第九十二条 阴谋颠覆政府、分裂国家的，处无期徒刑或者十年以上有期徒刑。

第九十三条 策动、勾引、收买国家工作人员、武装部队、人民警察、民兵投敌叛变或者叛乱的，处无期徒刑或者十年以上有期徒刑。

第九十四条 投敌叛变的，处三年以上十年以下有期徒刑；情节严重的或者率众投敌叛变的，处十年以上有期徒刑或者无期徒刑。

率领武装部队、人民警察、民兵投敌叛变的，处无期徒刑或者十年以上有期徒刑。

第九十五条 持械聚众叛乱的首要分子或者

其他罪恶重大的,处无期徒刑或者十年以上有期徒刑;其他积极参加的,处三年以上十年以下有期徒刑。

第九十六条 聚众劫狱或者组织越狱的首要分子或者其他罪恶重大的,处无期徒刑或者十年以上有期徒刑;其他积极参加的,处三年以上十年以下有期徒刑。

第九十七条 进行下列间谍或者资敌行为之一的,处十年以上有期徒刑或者无期徒刑;情节较轻的,处三年以上十年以下有期徒刑:

(一)为敌人窃取、刺探、提供情报的;

(二)供给敌人武器军火或者其他军用物资的;

(三)参加特务、间谍组织或者接受敌人派遣任务的。

第九十八条 组织、领导反革命集团的,处五年以上有期徒刑;其他积极参加反革命集团的,处五年以下有期徒刑、拘役、管制或者剥夺政治权利。

第九十九条 组织、利用封建迷信、会道门进行反革命活动的,处五年以上有期徒刑;情节较轻的,处五年以下有期徒刑、拘役、管制或者剥夺政治权利。

第一百条 以反革命为目的,进行下列破坏行为之一的，处无期徒刑或者十年以上有期徒刑；情节较轻的，处三年以上十年以下有期徒刑：

（一）爆炸、放火、决水、利用技术或者以其他方法破坏军事设备、生产设施、通讯交通设备、建筑工程、防险设备或者其他公共建设、公共财物的；

（二）抢劫国家档案、军事物资、工矿企业、银行、商店、仓库或者其他公共财物的；

（三）劫持船舰、飞机、火车、电车、汽车的；

（四）为敌人指示轰击目标的；

（五）制造、抢夺、盗窃枪支、弹药的。

第一百零一条 以反革命为目的，投放毒物、散布病菌或者以其他方法杀人、伤人的，处无期徒刑或者十年以上有期徒刑；情节较轻的，处三年以上十年以下有期徒刑。

第一百零二条 以反革命为目的，进行下列行为之一的，处五年以下有期徒刑、拘役、管制或者剥夺政治权利；首要分子或者其他罪恶重大的，处五年以上有期徒刑：

（一）煽动群众抗拒、破坏国家法律、法令实施的；

（二）以反革命标语、传单或者其他方法宣传煽动推翻无产阶级专政的政权和社会主义制度的。

第一百零三条 本章上述反革命罪行中，除第九十八条、第九十九条、第一百零二条外，对国家和人民危害特别严重、情节特别恶劣的，可以判处死刑。

第一百零四条 犯本章之罪的，可以并处没收财产。

第二章　危害公共安全罪

第一百零五条 放火、决水、爆炸或者以其他危险方法破坏工厂、矿场、油田、港口、河流、水源、仓库、住宅、森林、农场、谷场、牧场、重要管道、公共建筑物或者其他公私财产、危害公共安全，尚未造成严重后果的，处三年以上十年以下有期徒刑。

第一百零六条 放火、决水、爆炸、投毒或者以其他危险方法致人重伤、死亡或者使公私财产遭受重大损失的，处十年以上有期徒刑、无期徒刑或者死刑。

过失犯前款罪的，处七年以下有期徒刑或者拘役。

第一百零七条 破坏火车、汽车、电车、船只、飞机,足以使火车、汽车、电车、船只、飞机发生倾覆、毁坏危险,尚未造成严重后果的,处三年以上十年以下有期徒刑。

第一百零八条 破坏轨道、桥梁、隧道、公路、机场、航道、灯塔、标志或者进行其他破坏活动,足以使火车、汽车、电车、船只、飞机发生倾覆、毁坏危险,尚未造成严重后果的,处三年以上十年以下有期徒刑。

第一百零九条 破坏电力、煤气或者其他易燃易爆设备,危害公共安全,尚未造成严重后果的,处三年以上十年以下有期徒刑。

第一百一十条 破坏交通工具、交通设备、电力煤气设备、易燃易爆设备造成严重后果的,处十年以上有期徒刑、无期徒刑或者死刑。

过失犯前款罪的,处七年以下有期徒刑或者拘役。

第一百一十一条 破坏广播电台、电报、电话或者其他通讯设备,危害公共安全的,处七年以下有期徒刑或者拘役;造成严重后果的,处七年以上有期徒刑。

过失犯前款罪的,处七年以下有期徒刑或者拘役。

第一百一十二条 非法制造、买卖、运输枪支、弹药的,或者盗窃、抢夺国家机关、军警人员、民兵的枪支、弹药的,处七年以下有期徒刑;情节严重的,处七年以上有期徒刑或者无期徒刑。

第一百一十三条 从事交通运输的人员违反规章制度,因而发生重大事故,致人重伤、死亡或者使公私财产遭受重大损失的,处三年以下有期徒刑或者拘役;情节特别恶劣的,处三年以上七年以下有期徒刑。

非交通运输人员犯前款罪的,依照前款规定处罚。

第一百一十四条 工厂、矿山、林场、建筑企业或者其他企业、事业单位的职工,由于不服管理、违反规章制度,或者强令工人违章冒险作业,因而发生重大伤亡事故,造成严重后果的,处三年以下有期徒刑或者拘役;情节特别恶劣的,处三年以上七年以下有期徒刑。

第一百一十五条 违反爆炸性、易燃性、放射性、毒害性、腐蚀性物品的管理规定,在生产、储存、运输、使用中发生重大事故,造成严重后果的,处三年以下有期徒刑或者拘役;后果特别严重的,处三年以上七年以下有期徒刑。

第三章　破坏社会主义经济秩序罪

第一百一十六条　违反海关法规，进行走私，情节严重的，除按照海关法规没收走私物品并且可以罚款外，处三年以下有期徒刑或者拘役，可以并处没收财产。

第一百一十七条　违反金融、外汇、金银、工商管理法规，投机倒把，情节严重的，处三年以下有期徒刑或者拘役，可以并处、单处罚金或者没收财产。

第一百一十八条　以走私、投机倒把为常业的，走私、投机倒把数额巨大的或者走私、投机倒把集团的首要分子，处三年以上十年以下有期徒刑，可以并处没收财产。

第一百一十九条　国家工作人员利用职务上的便利，犯走私、投机倒把罪的，从重处罚。

第一百二十条　以营利为目的，伪造或者倒卖计划供应票证，情节严重的，处三年以下有期徒刑或者拘役，可以并处、单处罚金或者没收财产。

犯前款罪的首要分子或者情节特别严重的，处三年以上七年以下有期徒刑，可以并处没收财产。

第一百二十一条　违反税收法规，偷税、抗税，情节严重的，除按照税收法规补税并且可以罚款外，对直接责任人员，处三年以下有期徒刑或者拘役。

第一百二十二条　伪造国家货币或者贩运伪造的国家货币的，处三年以上七年以下有期徒刑，可以并处罚金或者没收财产。

犯前款罪的首要分子或者情节特别严重的，处七年以上有期徒刑或者无期徒刑，可以并处没收财产。

第一百二十三条　伪造支票、股票或者其他有价证券的，处七年以下有期徒刑，可以并处罚金。

第一百二十四条　以营利为目的，伪造车票、船票、邮票、税票、货票的，处二年以下有期徒刑、拘役或者罚金；情节严重的，处二年以上七年以下有期徒刑，可以并处罚金。

第一百二十五条　由于泄愤报复或者其他个人目的，毁坏机器设备、残害耕畜或者以其他方法破坏集体生产的，处二年以下有期徒刑或者拘役；情节严重的，处二年以上七年以下有期徒刑。

第一百二十六条　挪用国家救灾、抢险、防汛、优抚、救济款物，情节严重，致使国家和人民群众利益遭受重大损害的，对直接责任人员，处三年以下有期徒刑或者拘役；情节特别严重的，处三年以上七年以下有期徒刑。

第一百二十七条 违反商标管理法规，工商企业假冒其他企业已经注册的商标的，对直接责任人员，处三年以下有期徒刑、拘役或者罚金。

第一百二十八条 违反保护森林法规，盗伐、滥伐森林或者其他林木，情节严重的，处三年以下有期徒刑或者拘役，可以并处或者单处罚金。

第一百二十九条 违反保护水产资源法规，在禁渔区、禁渔期或者使用禁用的工具、方法捕捞水产品，情节严重的，处二年以下有期徒刑、拘役或者罚金。

第一百三十条 违反狩猎法规，在禁猎区、禁猎期或者使用禁用的工具、方法进行狩猎，破坏珍禽、珍兽或者其他野生动物资源，情节严重的，处二年以下有期徒刑、拘役或者罚金。

第四章　侵犯公民人身权利、　　　　　　民主权利罪

第一百三十一条 保护公民的人身权利、民主权利和其他权利，不受任何人、任何机关非法

侵犯。违法侵犯情节严重的，对直接责任人员予以刑事处分。

第一百三十二条 故意杀人的，处死刑、无期徒刑或者十年以上有期徒刑；情节较轻的，处三年以上十年以下有期徒刑。

第一百三十三条 过失杀人的，处五年以下有期徒刑；情节特别恶劣的，处五年以上有期徒刑。本法另有规定的，依照规定。

第一百三十四条 故意伤害他人身体的，处三年以下有期徒刑或者拘役。

犯前款罪，致人重伤的，处三年以上七年以下有期徒刑；致人死亡的，处七年以上有期徒刑或者无期徒刑。本法另有规定的，依照规定。

第一百三十五条 过失伤害他人致人重伤的，处二年以下有期徒刑或者拘役；情节特别恶劣的，处二年以上七年以下有期徒刑。本法另有规定的，依照规定。

第一百三十六条 严禁刑讯逼供。国家工作人员对人犯实行刑讯逼供的，处三年以下有期徒刑或者拘役。以肉刑致人伤残的，以伤害罪从重论处。

第一百三十七条 严禁聚众"打砸抢"。因"打砸抢"致人伤残、死亡的，以伤害罪、杀人罪论处。毁坏或者抢走公私财物的，除判令退赔外，首要分子以抢劫罪论处。

犯前款罪，可以单独判处剥夺政治权利。

第一百三十八条 严禁用任何方法、手段诬告陷害干部、群众。凡捏造事实诬告陷害他人（包括犯人）的，参照所诬陷的罪行的性质、情节、后果和量刑标准给予刑事处分。国家工作人员犯诬陷罪的，从重处罚。

不是有意诬陷，而是错告，或者检举失实的，不适用前款规定。

第一百三十九条 以暴力、胁迫或者其他手段强奸妇女的，处三年以上十年以下有期徒刑。

奸淫不满十四岁幼女的，以强奸论，从重处罚。

犯前两款罪，情节特别严重的或者致人重伤、死亡的，处十年以上有期徒刑、无期徒刑或者死刑。

二人以上犯强奸罪而共同轮奸的，从重处罚。

第一百四十条 强迫妇女卖淫的，处三年以上十年以下有期徒刑。

第一百四十一条 拐卖人口的，处五年以下有期徒刑；情节严重的，处五年以上有期徒刑。

第一百四十二条 违反选举法的规定，以暴力、威胁、欺骗、贿赂等非法手段破坏选举或者妨害选民自由行使选举权和被选举权的，处三年以下有期徒刑或者拘役。

第一百四十三条 严禁非法拘禁他人，或者以其他方法非法剥夺他人人身自由。违者处三年以下有期徒刑、拘役或者剥夺政治权利。具有殴打、侮辱情节的，从重处罚。

犯前款罪，致人重伤的，处三年以上十年以下有期徒刑；致人死亡的，处七年以上有期徒刑。

第一百四十四条 非法管制他人，或者非法搜查他人身体、住宅，或者非法侵入他人住宅的，处三年以下有期徒刑或者拘役。

第一百四十五条 以暴力或者其他方法，包括用"大字报"、"小字报"，公然侮辱他人或者捏造事实诽谤他人，情节严重的，处三年以下有期徒刑、拘役或者剥夺政治权利。

前款罪，告诉的才处理。但是严重危害社会秩序和国家利益的除外。

第一百四十六条 国家工作人员滥用职权、假公济私，对控告人、申诉人、批评人实行报复陷害的，处二年以下有期徒刑或者拘役；情节严重的，处二年以上七年以下有期徒刑。

第一百四十七条 国家工作人员非法剥夺公

民的正当的宗教信仰自由和侵犯少数民族风俗习惯，情节严重的，处二年以下有期徒刑或者拘役。

第一百四十八条 在侦查、审判中，证人、鉴定人、记录人、翻译人对与案件有重要关系的情节，故意作虚假证明、鉴定、记录、翻译，意图陷害他人或者隐匿罪证的，处二年以下有期徒刑或者拘役；情节严重的，处二年以上七年以下有期徒刑。

第一百四十九条 隐匿、毁弃或者非法开拆他人信件，侵犯公民通信自由权利，情节严重的，处一年以下有期徒刑或者拘役。

第五章　侵犯财产罪

第一百五十条 以暴力、胁迫或者其他方法抢劫公私财物的，处三年以上十年以下有期徒刑。

犯前款罪，情节严重的或者致人重伤、死亡的，处十年以上有期徒刑、无期徒刑或者死刑，可以并处没收财产。

第一百五十一条 盗窃、诈骗、抢夺公私财物数额较大的，处五年以下有期徒刑、拘役或者管制。

第一百五十二条 惯窃、惯骗或者盗窃、诈骗、抢夺公私财物数额巨大的,处五年以上十年以下有期徒刑;情节特别严重的,处十年以上有期徒刑或者无期徒刑,可以并处没收财产。

第一百五十三条 犯盗窃、诈骗、抢夺罪,为窝藏赃物、抗拒逮捕或者毁灭罪证而当场使用暴力或者以暴力相威胁的,依照本法第一百五十条抢劫罪处罚。

第一百五十四条 敲诈勒索公私财物的,处三年以下有期徒刑或者拘役;情节严重的,处三年以上七年以下有期徒刑。

第一百五十五条 国家工作人员利用职务上的便利,贪污公共财物的,处五年以下有期徒刑或者拘役;数额巨大、情节严重的,处五年以上有期徒刑;情节特别严重的,处无期徒刑或者死刑。

犯前款罪的,并处没收财产,或者判令退赔。

受国家机关、企业、事业单位、人民团体委托从事公务的人员犯第一款罪的,依照前两款的规定处罚。

第一百五十六条 故意毁坏公私财物,情节严重的,处三年以下有期徒刑、拘役或者罚金。

第六章　妨害社会管理秩序罪

第一百五十七条　以暴力、威胁方法阻碍国家工作人员依法执行职务的，或者拒不执行人民法院已经发生法律效力的判决、裁定的，处三年以下有期徒刑、拘役、罚金或者剥夺政治权利。

第一百五十八条　禁止任何人利用任何手段扰乱社会秩序。扰乱社会秩序情节严重，致使工作、生产、营业和教学、科研无法进行，国家和社会遭受严重损失的，对首要分子处五年以下有期徒刑、拘役、管制或者剥夺政治权利。

第一百五十九条　聚众扰乱车站、码头、民用航空站、商场、公园、影剧院、展览会、运动场或者其他公共场所秩序，聚众堵塞交通或者破坏交通秩序，抗拒、阻碍国家治安管理工作人员依法执行职务，情节严重的，对首要分子处五年以下有期徒刑、拘役、管制或者剥夺政治权利。

第一百六十条　聚众斗殴，寻衅滋事，侮辱妇女或者进行其他流氓活动，破坏公共秩序，情节恶劣的，处七年以下有期徒刑、拘役或者管制。

流氓集团的首要分子，处七年以上有期徒刑。

第一百六十一条　依法被逮捕、关押的犯罪分子脱逃的,除按其原犯罪行判处或者按其原判刑期执行外,加处五年以下有期徒刑或者拘役。

以暴力、威胁方法犯前款罪的,处二年以上七年以下有期徒刑。

第一百六十二条 窝藏或者作假证明包庇反革命分子的,处三年以下有期徒刑、拘役或者管制;情节严重的,处三年以上十年以下有期徒刑。

窝藏或者作假证明包庇其他犯罪分子的,处二年以下有期徒刑、拘役或者管制;情节严重的,处二年以上七年以下有期徒刑。

犯前两款罪,事前通谋的,以共同犯罪论处。

第一百六十三条 违反枪支管理规定,私藏枪支、弹药,拒不交出的,处二年以下有期徒刑或者拘役。

第一百六十四条 以营利为目的,制造、贩卖假药危害人民健康的,处二年以下有期徒刑、拘役或者管制,可以并处或者单处罚金;造成严重后果的,处二年以上七年以下有期徒刑,可以并处罚金。

第一百六十五条 神汉、巫婆借迷信进行造谣、诈骗财物活动的,处二年以下有期徒刑、拘役或者管制；情节严重的，处二年以上七年以下有期徒刑。

第一百六十六条 冒充国家工作人员招摇撞骗的，处三年以下有期徒刑、拘役、管制或者剥夺政治权利；情节严重的，处三年以上十年以下有期徒刑。

第一百六十七条 伪造、变造或者盗窃、抢夺、毁灭国家机关、企业、事业单位、人民团体的公文、证件、印章的，处三年以下有期徒刑、拘役、管制或者剥夺政治权利；情节严重的，处三年以上十年以下有期徒刑。

第一百六十八条 以营利为目的，聚众赌博或者以赌博为业的，处三年以下有期徒刑、拘役或者管制，可以并处罚金。

第一百六十九条 以营利为目的，引诱、容留妇女卖淫的，处五年以下有期徒刑、拘役或者管制；情节严重的，处五年以上有期徒刑，可以并处罚金或者没收财产。

第一百七十条 以营利为目的，制作、贩卖淫书、淫画的，处三年以下有期徒刑、拘役或者管制，可以并处罚金。

第一百七十一条 制造、贩卖、运输鸦片、海洛英、吗啡或者其他毒品的，处五年以下有期徒刑或者拘役，可以并处罚金。

一贯或者大量制造、贩卖、运输前款毒品的，处五年以上有期徒刑，可以并处没收财产。

第一百七十二条 明知是犯罪所得的赃物而予以窝藏或者代为销售的，处三年以下有期徒刑、拘役或者管制，可以并处或者单处罚金。

第一百七十三条 违反保护文物法规，盗运珍贵文物出口的，处三年以上十年以下有期徒刑，可以并处罚金；情节严重的，处十年以上有期徒刑或者无期徒刑，可以并处没收财产。

第一百七十四条 故意破坏国家保护的珍贵文物、名胜古迹的，处七年以下有期徒刑或者拘役。

第一百七十五条 故意破坏国家边境的界碑、界桩或者永久性测量标志的，处三年以下有期徒刑或者拘役。

以叛国为目的的，按照反革命罪处罚。

第一百七十六条 违反出入国境管理法规，偷越国（边）境，情节严重的，处一年以下有期徒刑、拘役或者管制。

第一百七十七条 以营利为目的，组织、运送他人偷越国（边）境的，处五年以下有期徒刑、拘役或者管制，可以并处罚金。

第一百七十八条 违反国境卫生检疫规定，引起检疫传染病的传播，或者有引起检疫传染病传播严重危险的，处三年以下有期徒刑或者拘役，可以并处或者单处罚金。

第七章 妨害婚姻、家庭罪

第一百七十九条 以暴力干涉他人婚姻自由的，处二年以下有期徒刑或者拘役。

犯前款罪，引起被害人死亡的，处二年以上七年以下有期徒刑。

第一款罪，告诉的才处理。

第一百八十条 有配偶而重婚的，或者明知他人有配偶而与之结婚的，处二年以下有期徒刑或者拘役。

第一百八十一条 明知是现役军人的配偶而与之同居或者结婚的，处三年以下有期徒刑。

第一百八十二条 虐待家庭成员，情节恶劣的，处二年以下有期徒刑、拘役或者管制。

犯前款罪，引起被害人重伤、死亡的，处二年以上七年以下有期徒刑。

第一款罪，告诉的才处理。

第一百八十三条 对于年老、年幼、患病或者其他没有独立生活能力的人，负有扶养义务而拒绝扶养,情节恶劣的,处五年以下有期徒刑、拘役或者管制。

第一百八十四条 拐骗不满十四岁的男、女,脱离家庭或者监护人的,处五年以下有期徒刑或者拘役。

第八章 渎职罪

第一百八十五条 国家工作人员利用职务上的便利,收受贿赂的,处五年以下有期徒刑或者拘役。赃款、赃物没收,公款、公物追还。

犯前款罪,致使国家或者公民利益遭受严重损失的,处五年以上有期徒刑。

向国家工作人员行贿或者介绍贿赂的,处三年以下有期徒刑或者拘役。

第一百八十六条 国家工作人员违反国家保密法规,泄露国家重要机密,情节严重的,处七年以下有期徒刑、拘役或者剥夺政治权利。

非国家工作人员犯前款罪的,依照前款的规定酌情处罚。

第一百八十七条 国家工作人员由于玩忽职守,致使公共财产、国家和人民利益遭受重大损失的,处五年以下有期徒刑或者拘役。

第一百八十八条 司法工作人员徇私舞弊,

对明知是无罪的人而使他受追诉、对明知是有罪的人而故意包庇不使他受追诉，或者故意颠倒黑白做枉法裁判的，处五年以下有期徒刑、拘役或者剥夺政治权利；情节特别严重的，处五年以上有期徒刑。

第一百八十九条 司法工作人员违反监管法规，对被监管人实行体罚虐待，情节严重的，处三年以下有期徒刑或者拘役；情节特别严重的，处三年以上十年以下有期徒刑。

第一百九十条 司法工作人员私放罪犯的，处五年以下有期徒刑或者拘役；情节严重的，处五年以上十年以下有期徒刑。

第一百九十一条 邮电工作人员私自开拆或者隐匿、毁弃邮件、电报的，处二年以下有期徒刑或者拘役。

犯前款罪而窃取财物的，依照第一百五十五条贪污罪从重处罚。

第一百九十二条 国家工作人员犯本章之罪，情节轻微的，可以由主管部门酌情予以行政处分。

THE CRIMINAL PROCEDURE LAW OF THE PEOPLE'S REPUBLIC OF CHINA

(Adopted by the Second Session of the Fifth National People's Congress, July 1, 1979 and Effective as of January 1, 1980)

CONTENTS

PART I GENERAL PROVISIONS 115

  Chapter I   Guiding Ideology, Tasks and Basic Principles 115

  Chapter II   Jurisdiction 118

  Chapter III   Withdrawal 121

  Chapter IV   Defence 122

  Chapter V   Evidence 123

  Chapter VI   Coercive Measures 125

  Chapter VII   Supplementary Civil Actions 131

  Chapter VIII   Time Periods and Service 131

  Chapter IX   Other Provisions 132

PART II FILING A CASE, INVESTIGATION AND INITIATION OF PUBLIC PROSECUTION 134

  Chapter I   Filing a Case 134

  Chapter II   Investigation 136

    Section 1 Interrogation of the Defendant 136
    Section 2 Questioning of the Witnesses 137
    Section 3 Inspection and Examination 138
    Section 4 Search 139
    Section 5 Seizure of Material Evidence and Documentary Evidence 140
    Section 6 Expert Evaluation 141
    Section 7 Wanted Orders 142
    Section 8 Conclusion of Investigation 142

  Chapter III   Initiation of Public Prosecution 143

PART III	**ADJUDICATION**	147
Chapter I	Organization of Adjudication	147
Chapter II	Procedure of First Instance	148
Section 1	Cases of Public Prosecution	148
Section 2	Cases of Private Prosecution	154
Chapter III	Procedure of Second Instance	155
Chapter IV	Procedure for Review of Death Sentences	160
Chapter V	Procedure for Adjudication Supervision	161
PART IV	**EXECUTION OF SENTENCES**	163

PART I GENERAL PROVISIONS

CHAPTER I GUIDING IDEOLOGY, TASKS AND BASIC PRINCIPLES

Article 1 The Criminal Procedure Law of the People's Republic of China, which takes Marxism-Leninism-Mao Zedong Thought as its guide and the Constitution as its basis, is formulated in light of the concrete experiences of all our country's ethnic groups in carrying out the people's democratic dictatorship led by the proletariat and based on the worker-peasant alliance, that is, the dictatorship of the proletariat, and the actual need to attack the enemy and protect the people.

Article 2 The tasks of the Criminal Procedure Law of the People's Republic of China are to guarantee the accurate and timely clarification of the facts of crimes, to apply the law correctly, to punish criminal elements, to safeguard innocent people from criminal prosecution, to educate citizens to observe the law voluntarily and to struggle against criminal conduct actively, in order to uphold the socialist legal system, to protect the rights of the person and the democratic rights and other rights of citizens, and to safeguard the smooth progress of the cause of socialist revolution and socialist construction.

Article 3 The public security organs are responsible for investigation, detention and preparatory examination in criminal cases. The people's procuratorates are responsible for approving arrest, conducting procuratorial work (including investigation) and initiating public prosecution. The people's courts are responsible for adjudication. No other organ, organization or individual has the right to exercise these powers.

In conducting criminal proceedings, the people's courts, the people's procuratorates and the public security organs must strictly observe this Law and relevant provisions of other laws.

Article 4 In conducting criminal proceedings, the people's courts, the people's procuratorates and the public security organs must rely on the masses and must take facts as the basis and law as the criterion. The law is equally applicable to all citizens, and no special privilege whatever is permissible before the law.

Article 5 In conducting criminal proceedings, the people's courts, the people's procuratorates and the public security organs shall have a division of labour with separate responsibilities and coordinate with each other and restrain each other in order to guarantee the accurate and effective enforcement of the law.

Article 6 Citizens of various ethnic groups all have the right to conduct proceedings in their native spoken and written language. The people's courts, the people's procuratorates and the public security organs shall provide interpretation for participants in proceedings who are not proficient in the spoken and written language commonly used in the locality.

In areas inhabited by a concentrated minority ethnic group or by several ethnic groups, hearings shall be carried out in the spoken language commonly used in the locality, and written judgments, announcements and other documents shall be issued in the written language commonly used in the locality.

Article 7 In adjudicating cases, the people's courts are to carry out a system in which the second instance is the final instance.

Article 8 The people's courts are to adjudicate all cases in public unless otherwise provided by this Law. Defendants have the right to obtain defence, and the people's courts have the duty to guarantee that defendants obtain defence.

Article 9 In adjudicating cases, the people's courts, in accordance with this Law, are to carry out the system of people's assessors taking part in adjudication.

Article 10 The people's courts, the people's procuratorates and the public security organs shall safeguard the procedural rights that participants in proceedings enjoy according to law.

In cases in which a minor under the age of eighteen commits a crime, the legal representative of the defendant may be notified to be present at the time of interrogation and adjudication.

Participants in proceedings have the right to bring complaints against adjudication personnel, procuratorial personnel and investigation personnel for acts that violate their procedural rights as citizens and that subject their persons to indignities.

Article 11 In any of the following circumstances,

criminal responsibility is not to be investigated, or, in situations where investigation has already been undertaken, the case shall be quashed, or there shall be no prosecution, or an announcement of not guilty shall be made:

1. If the circumstances are clearly minor, the harm is not great, and the act is thus not deemed to be a crime;

2. If the period of limitation for prosecuting the crime has expired;

3. If an exemption from criminal punishment has been ordered in a special amnesty decree;

4. If, according to the Criminal Law, a crime is to be handled only upon complaint and there has been no complaint or the complaint has been withdrawn;

5. If the defendant is deceased; or

6. If other laws or decrees provide for exemption from investigation of criminal responsibility.

Article 12 In cases where foreigners commit crimes and criminal responsibility should be investigated, the provisions of this Law are to be applicable.

Cases where foreigners with diplomatic privileges and immunity commit crimes and criminal responsibility should be investigated are to be resolved through diplomatic channels.

CHAPTER II JURISDICTION

Article 13 Minor criminal cases that may be handled only upon complaint and others that do not require the conducting of an investigation are to be accepted directly by the people's courts, and mediation may be carried out.

Cases involving crimes of corruption, violation of the democratic rights of citizens, and dereliction of duty, and other cases that the people's procuratorates consider necessary directly to accept themselves are to be filed and investigated by the people's procuratorates, which are to decide whether or not to initiate a public prosecution.

The investigation of cases other than those provided in the first and second paragraphs are all to be conducted by the public security organs.

Article 14 The basic people's courts have jurisdiction as courts of first instance over ordinary criminal cases, with the exception of those cases over which people's courts at higher levels have jurisdiction according to this Law.

Article 15 The intermediate people's courts have jurisdiction as courts of first instance over the following criminal cases:

1. Counterrevolutionary cases;
2. Ordinary criminal cases in which there may be a sentence of life imprisonment or death; and
3. Criminal cases in which foreigners commit crimes or in which citizens of our country violate the lawful rights of foreigners.

Article 16 Criminal cases over which the high people's courts have jurisdiction as courts of first instance are major criminal cases with an impact on an entire province (municipality directly under the central government, or autonomous region).

Article 17 Criminal cases over which the Supreme People's Court has jurisdiction as the court of first instance are major criminal cases with an impact on the entire country.

Article 18 When necessary, people's courts at higher levels may adjudicate cases over which people's courts at lower levels have jurisdiction as courts of first instance; they may also transfer criminal cases over which they themselves have jurisdiction as courts of first instance to people's courts at lower levels for adjudication; people's courts at lower levels, when they consider the circumstances of a criminal case in the first instance to be major or complex and to require adjudication by a people's court at a higher level, may request that the case be transferred to a people's court at the next level up for adjudication.

Article 19 A criminal case is under the jurisdiction of the people's court in the place where the crime was committed. If it is more appropriate for the people's court in the place of the defendant's residence to adjudicate the case, jurisdiction may be taken by the people's court in the place of the defendant's residence.

Article 20 Cases over which several people's courts at the same level have jurisdiction are to be adjudicated by the people's court that first accepted the case. When necessary, such cases may be transferred for adjudication to the people's court in the principal place of the crime.

Article 21 People's courts at higher levels may instruct people's courts at lower levels to adjudicate cases over which jurisdiction is unclear and may also instruct people's courts at lower levels to transfer cases to other people's courts for adjudication.

Article 22 Stipulations are to be made separately for jurisdiction over cases in special people's courts.

CHAPTER III WITHDRAWAL

Article 23 In any of the following circumstances, a member of the adjudication personnel, procuratorial personnel and investigation personnel shall withdraw of his own accord, and parties and their legal representatives also have the right to demand his withdrawal:

1. If he is a party or close relative of a party to the case;
2. If he himself or his close relative has an interest in the case;
3. If he has served as a witness, expert witness or defender in the case or as a representative of a party to a supplementary civil action; or
4. If he has another relationship with a party to the case that may influence the just handling of the case.

Article 24 The withdrawal of adjudication personnel, procuratorial personnel and investigation personnel shall be decided respectively by the president of the court, the chief procurator and the responsible person in the public security organ; the withdrawal of the president of the court is to be decided by the adjudication committee of that court; the withdrawal of the chief procurator and of the responsible person in the public security organ is to be decided by the procuratorial committee of the people's procuratorate at the same level.

Investigation personnel may not cease their investigation of a case before a decision is rendered on their withdrawal.

Where a decision is made to reject an application for withdrawal, a party may apply for one reconsideration.

Article 25 The provisions of Article 23 and Article 24 of this Law are also applicable to clerks, interpreters and expert witnesses.

CHAPTER IV   DEFENCE

Article 26 In addition to exercising the right to defend themselves, defendants may also authorize the following people to defend them:

1. Lawyers;

2. Citizens who are recommended by a people's organization or by the defendant's unit or who are authorized by the people's court; and

3. Close relatives or guardians of the defendant.

Article 27 In cases in which a public prosecutor appears in court to bring a public prosecution, and the defendant has not authorized anyone to be his defender, the people's court may designate a defender for the defendant.

In cases in which the defendant is deaf, mute or a minor and has not authorized anyone to be his defender, the people's court shall designate a defender for him.

Article 28 The responsibility of a defender is, on the basis of the facts and the law, to present materials and opinions proving that the defendant is innocent, that his crime is minor, or that he should receive a mitigated punishment or be exempted from criminal responsibility, safeguarding the lawful rights and interests of the defendant.

Article 29 A defence lawyer may consult the materials of the case, acquaint himself with the circumstances of the case, and may interview and correspond with a defendant held in custody; other defenders, with the permission of the people's court, may also acquaint themselves with the circumstances of the case and interview and correspond with a defendant held in custody.

Article 30 During the adjudication process, a defendant may refuse to have a defender continue to defend him and may also authorize another defender to defend him.

CHAPTER V   EVIDENCE

Article 31 All facts that prove the true circumstances of a case are evidence.

There are the following six categories of evidence:
1. Material evidence and documentary evidence;
2. Testimony of witnesses;
3. Statements of victims;
4. Statements and exculpations of defendants;
5. Conclusions of expert evaluations; and
6. Transcripts of inspection and examination.

The above evidence must be verified before it can be used as the basis for determining cases.

Article 32 Adjudication personnel, procuratorial personnel and investigation personnel must, in accordance with legally-prescribed procedures, gather various types of evidence that can prove the defendant's guilt or innocence and the gravity of the circumstances of the crime. The use of torture to coerce statements and the gathering of evidence by threat, enticement, deceit or other unlawful methods are strictly prohibited. Conditions must be guaranteed for all citizens who are involved in the case or who are acquainted with the circumstances of the case to provide evidence objectively and fully, and, except in special circumstances, they may be brought in to assist in the investigation.

Article 33 Applications for approval of arrest submitted by the public security organs, bills of prosecution of the people's procuratorates and judgments of the people's courts must be faithful to the facts and the true situation. The responsibility of those who intentionally conceal the facts and the true situation shall be investigated.

Article 34 The people's courts, the people's procuratorates and the public security organs have the right to gather and obtain evidence from the relevant state organs, enterprises, institutions, people's communes, people's organizations and citizens.

Evidence involving state secrets shall be kept secret.

Anyone who falsifies, conceals or destroys evidence, regardless of which side he belongs to, must be investigated under the law.

Article 35 In the decision of all cases, the emphasis should be placed on evidence and investigative research, and credence should not be readily given to oral statements. In cases where there is only the statement of the defendant and there is no other evidence, the defendant cannot be found guilty and sentenced to a criminal punishment; in cases where there is no statement of the defendant and the evidence is complete and reliable, the defendant may be found guilty and sentenced to a criminal punishment.

Article 36 The testimony of witnesses must be subjected in the courtroom to the questioning and cross-examination of both sides — the public prosecutor and the victim, and the defendant and the defender — and only after the testimony of witnesses on all sides has been heard and has undergone verification may it be used as a basis for determining a case. Should the tribunal ascertain that a witness has intentionally given false testimony or concealed criminal evidence, it shall handle the matter according to law.

Article 37 Anyone with knowledge about the circumstances of the case has the duty to testify.

Those with physical or mental handicaps or those of a young age who cannot distinguish right from wrong or cannot accurately express themselves cannot be witnesses.

CHAPTER VI COERCIVE MEASURES

Article 38 The people's courts, the people's procuratorates and the public security organs, according to the circumstances of the case, may summon a defendant for detention, allow him to obtain a guarantor and await trial out of custody, or allow him to live at home under surveillance.

A defendant who lives at home under surveillance may not leave the designated area. Surveillance of his home is to be carried out by the local public security station or by the people's commune or the defendant's unit entrusted with the task.

In cases where the defendant is allowed to obtain a guarantor and await trial out of custody or to live at home under surveillance, if changes in the circumstances develop, these measures shall be revoked or altered.

Article 39 The arrest of an offender must be approved by a people's procuratorate or decided by a people's court and is to be carried out by a public security organ.

Article 40 In the case of an offender the principal facts of whose crime have already been clarified and who could be sentenced to a punishment of not less than imprisonment, where adopting such measures as allowing him to obtain a guarantor and await trial out of custody or to live at home under surveillance would be insufficient to prevent the occurrence of danger to society and where there is thus the necessity of arrest, the offender shall be immediately arrested according to law.

In the case of an offender who should be arrested but who is suffering from grave illness or is a woman who is pregnant or nursing her own baby, the measures of allowing the person to obtain a guarantor and await trial out of custody or to live at home under surveillance may be adopted.

Article 41 In any of the following circumstances, the public security organs may first detain an active criminal who, on the basis of his crime, should be arrested, or a major suspect element:

1. If he is in the process of preparing to commit a crime, is committing a crime or is discovered immediately after committing a crime;

2. If he is identified as having committed a crime by the victim or by an eyewitness on the scene;

3. If he is discovered to have criminal evidence on his person or at his residence;

4. If, after committing the crime, he attempts to commit suicide or to escape or is a fugitive;

5. If he may possible destroy or falsify evidence or collude with others to devise a consistent story;

6. If his identity is unclear and there is strong suspicion that he is a person who goes from place to place committing crimes; or

7. If he is carrying on "beating, smashing and looting" and gravely undermining work, production or social order.

Article 42 With respect to the following offenders, any citizen may seize them and deliver them to the public security organs, the people's procuratorates or the people's courts for handling:

1. Those who are in the process of committing a crime or are discovered immediately after committing a crime;

2. Those who are wanted for arrest;

3. Those who have escaped from prison; and

4. Those who are being pursued for arrest.

Article 43 When a public security organ detains a person, it must produce a detention warrant.

The family of the detained person or his unit shall be notified within twenty-four hours after detention of the reasons for detention and the place of custody, except in circumstances where notification would hinder the investigation or there is no way to notify them.

Article 44 The public security organ shall conduct interrogation of the detained person within twenty-four hours after detention. When it is discovered that he should not have been detained, the detained person must be released immediately and be issued a release certificate. A person whom it is necessary to arrest but against whom there is not yet sufficient evidence may be allowed to obtain a guarantor and await trial out of custody or to live at home under surveillance.

Article 45 When a public security organ wishes to arrest an offender, it shall write out a proposal for approval of arrest which, together with the materials in the case file and the evidence, is to be transferred to the people's procuratorate at the same level for review and approval. Where necessary, the people's procuratorate may send people to participate in the discussion of a major case by the public security organ.

Article 46 When a people's procuratorate reviews and approves the arrest of an offender, the chief procurator shall make the decision. A major case shall be submitted to the procuratorial committee for discussion and decision.

Article 47 After conducting a review of a case that a public security organ has submitted for approval of arrest, the people's procuratorate, according to the differing circumstances, shall make a decision to approve arrest, not to approve arrest, or to have supplementary investigation.

Article 48 In cases where a public security organ considers it necessary to arrest a detained person, it shall, within three days after detention, submit a request to the people's procuratorate for review and approval. Under special circumstances, the time for requesting review and approval may be extended by from one to four days. The people's procuratorate shall make its decision to approve arrest or not to approve arrest within three days after receiving the application for approval of arrest from the public security organ. In cases where the people's procuratorate does not approve the arrest, the public security organ shall, immediately after receiving the notice, release the detained person and issue him a release certificate.

If the public security organ or the people's procuratorate has not handled a matter in accordance with the provisions of the preceding paragraph, the detained person or his family has the right to demand release, and the public security organ or the people's procuratorate shall immediately release him.

Article 49 When a public security organ considers that a decision of the people's procuratorate not to approve arrest is mistaken, it may demand reconsideration, but it must immediately release the detained person. If its opinion is not accepted, it may request review by the people's procuratorate at the next level up. The higher-level people's procuratorate shall immediately review the matter, render a decision whether or not to make any revision, and inform the people's procuratorate and the public security organ at the lower level to carry out the decision.

Article 50 When a public security organ arrests a person, it must produce an arrest warrant.

The family of the arrested person or his unit shall be notified within twenty-four hours after arrest of the reasons for arrest and the place of custody, except in circumstances where notification would hinder the investigation or there is no way to notify them.

Article 51 Interrogation must be conducted within twenty-four hours after arrest, by a people's court or a people's procuratorate with respect to a person it has decided on its own to arrest, and by a public security organ with respect to a person it has arrested with the approval of a people's procuratorate. When it is discovered that the person should not have been arrested, he must be released immediately and issued a release certificate.

Article 52 If in the course of its work of reviewing and approving arrests, a people's procuratorate discovers that there are illegalities in the investigation activities of a public security organ, it shall notify the public security organ to rectify them, and the public security organ shall notify the people's procuratorate of the circumstances of the correction.

CHAPTER VII SUPPLEMENTARY CIVIL ACTIONS

Article 53 A victim who has suffered material losses because of the defendant's criminal act has the right, during the process of criminal procedure, to bring a supplementary civil action.

If it is state property or collective property that has suffered losses, a people's procuratorate, when initiating a public prosecution, may bring a supplementary civil action.

When necessary, a people's court may seal up or seize the defendant's property.

Article 54 A supplementary civil action shall be adjudicated together with the criminal case. Only for the purpose of preventing excessive delay in adjudication of the criminal case may the same adjudication organization, after the criminal case has been adjudicated, continue to hear the supplementary civil action.

CHAPTER VIII TIME PERIODS AND SERVICE

Article 55 Time periods are counted in hours, days and months.

The hour and day in which a time period begins are not counted as within that time period.

Legally-prescribed time periods do not include travel time. Appeals or other documents that have been posted before the expiration of the time period are not to be considered overdue.

Article 56 In cases where parties are delayed and cannot meet the deadline because of irresistible causes or other legitimate reasons, they may, within five days after the removal of the obstacle, apply to continue conducting the procedural activities that should have been completed before the expiration of the time period.

The people's court is to issue an order on whether or not to approve the application in the preceding paragraph.

Article 57 The service of subpoenas, notices and other procedural documents shall be made upon the addressee himself; if the person is not in, delivery may be made on his behalf to an adult member of his family or a responsible person of his unit.

When the addressee himself or the person receiving on his behalf refuses to accept a document or refuses to sign his name or place his seal upon a document, the person serving the document may invite the addressee's neighbour or other eyewitness to the scene, explain the situation, leave the document at his residence, record on the service certificate the particulars of refusal and the date of service and then put his own signature to it. The service is thus to be deemed to have been made.

CHAPTER IX OTHER PROVISIONS

Article 58 The meanings of the following terms used in this Law are:

1. "Investigation" refers to the specialized investigatory work conducted and the related coercive

measures taken according to law by the public security organs and the people's procuratorates in the process of handling cases;

2. "Parties" refers to private prosecutors, defendants, and plaintiffs and defendants in supplementtary civil actions;

3. "Legal representatives" refers to the parents, adoptive parents or guardians of the person represented and the representatives of an organ or organization that has the responsibility to provide protection;

4. "Participants in proceedings" refers to parties, victims, legal representatives, defenders, witnesses, expert witnesses and interpreters; and

5. "Close relatives" refers to husbands, wives, fathers, mothers, sons, daughters, and brothers and sisters born of the same parents.

PART II FILING A CASE, INVESTIGATION AND INITIATION OF PUBLIC PROSECUTION

CHAPTER I FILING A CASE

Article 59 Upon discovery of facts of a crime or criminal suspects, state organs, organizations, enterprises, institutions and citizens have the right and also the duty to bring complaints and accusations to the public security organs, the people's procuratorates and the people's courts, within the scope of jurisdiction provided in Article 13 of this Law.

The public security organs, the people's procuratorates and the people's courts shall accept complaints, accusations and the voluntary surrender of criminals. In cases where the matter does not fall under the jurisdiction of the organ receiving it, that organ shall transfer it to the competent organ for handling and notify the complainant and accuser; in cases where the matter does not fall under the jurisdiction of the organ receiving it but where emergency measures must be adopted, emergency measures shall first be adopted and the matter then transferred to the competent organ.

Article 60 Complaints and accusations may be submitted in written or oral form. Personnel who receive oral complaints and accusations shall make a written transcript that the complainant or accuser is to sign or place his seal upon after it has been read to him and found free of error.

Personnel who accept complaints and accusations shall explain to complainants and accusers the legal responsibility to be incurred for false accusations. However, so long as fabrication of facts and fabrication of evidence are not involved, cases where a complaint or an accusation is at variance with the facts and even cases of mistaken complaints are to be strictly distinguished from false accusations.

If the complainant or accuser does not want to make his own name public, during the investigation period it shall be kept secret for him.

Article 61 The people's courts, the people's procuratorates and the public security organs shall, in accordance with the scope of their jurisdiction, promptly conduct a review of the materials involved in complaints, accusations and voluntary surrenders, and if they believe that there are facts of a crime necessitating the investigation of criminal responsibility, they shall file a case; if they believe that there are no facts of a crime or that the facts of a crime are obviously minor and do not necessitate the investigation of criminal responsibility, they are not to file a case, and they will inform the complainant of the reasons for not filing a case. If the complainant does not agree, he may apply for reconsideration.

CHAPTER II INVESTIGATION

SECTION 1 INTERROGATION OF THE DEFENDANT

Article 62 The responsibility for conducting interrogation of the defendant must be borne by the investigation personnel of the people's procuratorates or the public security organs. No fewer than two investigation personnel may be present during interrogation.

Article 63 A defendant whom it is not necessary to arrest or detain may be summoned to a designated place for interrogation, or the interrogation may be conducted at his residence or his unit, but he shall be shown a certificate of a people's procuratorate or a public security organ.

Article 64 When interrogating a defendant, investigation personnel shall first ask the defendant whether or not he has engaged in a criminal act and let him state the circumstances of his guilt or explain his innocence, and then put questions to him. The defendant shall answer the questions put by the investigation personnel according to the facts. However, he has the right to refuse to answer questions that have no relation to the case.

Article 65 A person who is proficient in sign language shall participate in the interrogation of a deaf or mute defendant, and a clear transcript is to be made of such circumstances.

Article 66 The transcript of the interrogation shall be turned over to the defendant for checking, and it shall be read to a defendant who is unable to read. If there are omissions or errors in the record, the defendant may present additions or corrections. After the defendant has acknowledged that the transcript is free of error, he shall sign it or place his seal upon it. The investigation personnel shall also sign the transcript. If the defendant asks to write a statement himself, he shall be permitted to do so. When necessary, investigation personnel may also request the defendant to make a written statement in his own handwriting.

SECTION 2 QUESTIONING OF THE WITNESSES

Article 67 Investigation personnel may question a witness at his unit or residence, but they must produce a certificate of a people's procuratorate or a public security organ. When necessary, they may also notify witnesses to come to the people's procuratorate or the public security organ to provide testimony.

Witnesses shall be questioned individually.

Article 68 When a witness is questioned, he shall be told that he shall provide evidence and testimony according to the facts and of the legal responsibility to be incurred for intentionally giving false testimony or concealing criminal evidence.

Article 69 The provisions of Article 66 of this Law also apply to the questioning of witnesses.

Article 70 In the questioning of victims, the provisions of the various articles of this section are to be applied.

SECTION 3 INSPECTION AND EXAMINATION

Article 71 Investigation personnel shall conduct inspection or examination of sites, articles, persons and corpses related to a crime. When necessary, people with specialized knowledge may be assigned or invited to conduct inspection or examination under the direction of investigation personnel.

Article 72 Every unit and individual has the duty to protect the scene of a crime and immediately to inform the public security organs to send personnel to inspect it.

Article 73 To conduct inspection or examination, investigation personnel must hold a certificate of a public security organ.

Article 74 The public security organs have the right to decide on an autopsy of the corpse where the cause of death is not clear and to inform the family members of the deceased to be present.

Article 75 Examination of the persons of victims or defendants may be conducted in order to ascertain certain of their characteristics, the circumstances of their injuries or their physiological condition.

If a defendant refuses to be examined, the investigation personnel, when they consider it necessary, may compel examination.

Examination of the persons of women shall be conducted by female personnel or physicians.

Article 76 A transcript of the circumstances of inspection or examination shall be made, and those who participate in the inspection or examination and the eyewitnesses shall sign it or place their seals upon it.

Article 77 When in reviewing a case a people's procuratorate considers that reinspection or reexamination of the inspection or examination done by a public security organ is necessary, it may demand that the public security organ conduct a reinspection or reexamination, and it may also send procuratorial personnel to participate.

Article 78 In order to clarify the circumstances of a case, when necessary, investigative experiments may be conducted with the approval of the chief of a public security bureau.

In investigative experiments, all acts capable of causing danger, insulting human dignity or offending public morals are prohibited.

SECTION 4 SEARCH

Article 79 For the purpose of gathering criminal evidence and apprehending criminals, investigation personnel may conduct searches of the persons, articles, residences and other relevant places of defendants and people who might conceal criminals or criminal evidence.

Article 80 Every unit and individual has a duty, on the demand of people's procuratorates and public security organs, to turn over material evidence and documentary evidence that may prove the guilt or innocence of a defendant.

Article 81 In conducting a search, a search warrant must be shown to the person searched.

When carrying out arrest or detention, if an

emergency situation is encountered, a search may be conducted without the use of a search warrant.

Article 82 The person searched or his family members, neighbours or other eyewitnesses shall be present during a search.

Searches of the persons of women shall be conducted by female personnel.

Article 83 A transcript shall be made of the circumstances of a search, and the investigation personnel and the person searched or his family members, neighbours or other eyewitnesses shall sign it or place their seals upon it. If the person searched or his family members are fugitives or refuse to sign or place their seals upon the transcript, this shall be noted on the transcript.

SECTION 5 SEIZURE OF MATERIAL EVIDENCE AND DOCUMENTARY EVIDENCE

Article 84 All kinds of articles and documents discovered in inspections or searches that may be used to prove the guilt or innocence of a defendant shall be seized; articles and documents that have no relation to the case may not be seized.

Seized articles and documents should be well cared for or sealed up for safekeeping; they may not be used or damaged.

Article 85 The number of seized articles and documents shall be checked clearly in the company of the eyewitnesses present and the holder of the seized articles; an inventory shall be made in duplicate on the spot; the investigation personnel, the eyewitnesses and the holder shall sign it or place their seals upon it; and one copy shall be given to the holder and another copy placed on file for reference.

Article 86 When investigation personnel consider it necessary to seize the mail or telegrams of a defendant, upon approval of a public security organ or a people's procuratorate, they may notify the post and telecommunications organ to check for relevant mail and telegrams and turn them over to the investigation personnel for seizure.

When it is not necessary to continue seizure, the post and telecommunications organ shall be notified immediately.

Article 87 When it has been ascertained that seized articles, documents, mail or telegrams actually have no relation to the case, they shall be promptly returned to the original owner or to the original post and telecommunications organ.

SECTION 6 EXPERT EVALUATION

Article 88 When it is necessary, in order to clarify the circumstances of a case, to solve certain problems of a specialized nature in the case, persons with specialized knowledge shall be assigned or invited to conduct expert evaluation.

Article 89 After conducting an expert evaluation, experts shall write and sign a conclusion of expert evaluation.

Article 90 A defendant shall be informed of a conclusion of expert evaluation that is to be used as evidence. A supplementary expert evaluation or a new expert evaluation may be made if the defendant makes application for one.

SECTION 7 WANTED ORDERS

Article 91 If a defendant who should be arrested is a fugitive, the public security organs may issue a wanted order and adopt effective measures to pursue him for arrest and bring him to justice.

Public security organs at various levels may directly issue wanted orders within the area of their own jurisdiction; beyond the area of their own jurisdiction, they shall request the higher-level organs that have the decision-making authority to issue them.

SECTION 8 CONCLUSION OF INVESTIGATION

Article 92 The period for holding a defendant in custody during investigation may not exceed two months. Where the circumstances of a case are complex and the case cannot be concluded before the expiration of the period, the period may be extended by one month with the approval of the people's procuratorate at the next level up.

In the event of an especially major or complex case that still cannot be concluded after an extension according to the provisions of the preceding paragraph, the Supreme People's Procuratorate shall request the Standing Committee of the National People's Congress to approve postponement of the hearing of the case.*

Article 93 In a case investigated by a people's procuratorate, after conclusion of the investigation, it shall make a decision to initiate a public prosecution, to exempt from prosecution or to quash the case.

In a case investigated by a public security organ, after conclusion of the investigation, it shall draft an opinion recommending prosecution or an opinion recommending exemption from prosecution and transfer it together with the materials in the case file and the evidence to the people's procuratorate at the same level for review and decision.

Article 94 If in the process of investigation, it is discovered that the defendant's criminal responsibility should not be investigated, the case shall be quashed; if the defendant has already been arrested, he shall be immediately released and issued a release certificate, and the people's procuratorate that originally approved the arrest is to be notified.

CHAPTER III INITIATION OF PUBLIC PROSECUTION

Article 95 A people's procuratorate shall review and make a decision in all cases in which it is neces-

---

* Extension of time limits for handling cases was stipulated in a decision of the Standing Committee of the National People's Congress, September 10, 1981. *See* pp. 226-27 below. — *Trans.*

sary to initiate a public prosecution or to exempt from prosecution.

Article 96 In reviewing cases, a people's procuratorate must ascertain:

1. Whether the facts and circumstances of the crime are clear, whether the evidence is reliable and complete and whether the nature of the crime and the charge are correctly determined;

2. Whether there are crimes that have been omitted and whether there are other persons whose criminal responsibility should be investigated;

3. Whether it is a case in which criminal responsibility should not be investigated;

4. Whether there is a supplementary civil action; and

5. Whether the investigation activities were lawful.

Article 97 A people's procuratorate shall render a decision within one month with respect to cases that the public security organs transfer with a recommendation to initiate a public prosecution or to exempt from prosecution; in major or complex cases there may be an extension of one-half month.*

Article 98 In reviewing a case, a people's procuratorate shall interrogate the defendant.

Article 99 In reviewing a case that requires supplementary investigation, a people's procuratorate may investigate on its own and may also return the case to the public security organ for supplementary investigation.

In cases where there is supplementary investiga-

---

* See note to Article 92, *supra*. — *Trans.*

tion, supplementary investigation shall be completed within one month.

Article 100 In cases where a people's procuratorate considers that the facts of the defendant's crime have already been clarified, that the evidence is reliable and complete and that according to law criminal responsibility should be investigated, it shall make a decision to prosecute and initiate a public prosecution in a people's court in accordance with the provisions on adjudication jurisdiction.

Article 101 In cases where, according to the provisions of the Criminal Law, it is not necessary to impose a sentence of criminal punishment or an exemption from criminal punishment may be granted, a people's procuratorate may grant exemption from prosecution.

Article 102 A decision to exempt from prosecution shall be publicly announced and the written decision to exempt from prosecution shall be given to the defendant and to his unit. If the defendant is in custody, he shall be immediately released.

When a people's procuratorate decides to exempt from prosecution a case that a public security organ has transferred for prosecution, it shall deliver the document of decision to exempt from prosecution to the public security organ. When the public security organ considers that a decision to exempt from prosecution is mistaken, it may demand reconsideration, and if its opinion is not accepted, it may request review by the people's procuratorate at the next level up.

When there is a decision to exempt from prosecution a case in which there is a victim, the people's procuratorate shall deliver the document of decision to exempt from prosecution to the victim. If the victim does not agree, he may, within seven days after receipt, petition the people's procuratorate. The people's procuratorate shall inform the victim of the result of its reexamination.

Article 103 If a defendant does not agree with the decision to exempt the case from prosecution, he may, within seven days, petition the people's procuratorate. The people's procuratorate shall make a decision on reexamination, inform the defendant and at the same time send a copy of the decision to the public security organ.

Article 104 If any of the circumstances provided in Article 11 of this Law is applicable to the defendant, the people's procuratorate shall make a decision not to prosecute.

The provisions of Article 102 of this Law apply to decisions not to prosecute.

PART III ADJUDICATION

CHAPTER I ORGANIZATION OF ADJUDICATION

Article 105 Adjudication of cases in the first instance in the basic people's courts and the intermediate people's courts shall be conducted by a collegial panel composed of one judge and two people's assessors, with the exception of cases of private prosecution and other minor criminal cases that a single judge may adjudicate on his own.

Adjudication of cases in the first instance in the high people's courts or the Supreme People's Court shall be conducted by a collegial panel composed of from one to three judges and from two to four people's assessors.

In carrying out their duties in the people's courts, people's assessors have equal rights with judges.

Adjudication of appealed and protested cases in the people's courts shall be conducted by a collegial panel composed of from three to five judges.

The president of the court or the president of a chamber is to designate one judge to serve as chief judge of the collegial panel. When the president of the court or the president of a chamber participates in the adjudication of a case, he himself is to serve as chief judge.

Article 106 When the collegial panel is conducting its deliberations, if opinions diverge, the minority shall defer to the majority, but the opinion of the minority shall be entered in the transcript. The transcript of the deliberations is to be signed by the members of the collegial panel.

Article 107 All major or difficult cases, where the president of the court considers it necessary to submit the matter to the adjudication committee for discussion, are to be submitted by the president of the court to the adjudication committee for discussion and decision. The collegial panel shall carry out decisions of the adjudication committee.

CHAPTER II PROCEDURE OF FIRST INSTANCE

SECTION 1 CASES OF PUBLIC PROSECUTION

Article 108 After a people's court has conducted a review of a case in which a public prosecution has been initiated, where the facts of the crime are clear and the evidence is complete, it shall decide to open the court session and adjudicate the case; where the principal facts are not clear and the evidence is insufficient, it may remand the case to the people's procuratorate for supplementary investigation; where there is no need for a criminal sentence, it may demand that the people's procuratorate withdraw its prosecution.

Article 109 When necessary, the people's court may conduct inspection, examination, search, seizure and expert evaluation.

Article 110 After the people's court has decided to open the court session and adjudicate the case, it shall proceed with the following work:

1. Determining the members of the collegial panel;

2. Delivering to the defendant, no later than seven days before opening the court session, a copy of the bill of prosecution of the people's procuratorate, and informing the defendant that he may appoint a defender, or, when necessary, designating a defender for the defendant;

3. Informing the people's procuratorate, three days before opening the court session, of the time and place of the court session;

4. Summoning the parties, notifying defenders, witnesses, expert witnesses and interpreters, and delivering the subpoenas and notices no later than three days before the opening of the court session; and

5. In cases to be adjudicated in public, announcing in advance the subject matter of the case, the name of the defendant, and the time and place of the court session.

The circumstances of the above activities shall be entered in the transcript, which is to be signed by the adjudication personnel and court clerk.*

---

* The procedures of Article 110 have been modified by the Decision of the Standing Committee of the National People's Congress Regarding the Procedure for Rapid Adjudication of Cases Involving Criminal Elements Who Seriously Endanger Public Security. *See* pp. 239-40 below. — *Trans.*

Article 111 The people's courts shall conduct adjudication of cases in the first instance in public. However, cases involving state secrets or the private affairs of individuals are not to be heard in public.

No cases involving the commission of crimes by minors aged fourteen or over but under the age of sixteen are to be heard in public. Cases involving the commission of crimes by minors aged sixteen or over but under the age of eighteen are also generally not to be heard in public.

In a case that is not to be heard in public, the reasons for not hearing it in public shall be announced in court.

Article 112 When a people's court adjudicates a case of public prosecution, the people's procuratorate shall send personnel to appear in court to support the public prosecution, except in cases where the criminal conduct is relatively minor and the people's court has agreed for personnel not to be sent.

When the procuratorial personnel appearing in court discover that there are illegalities in the adjudication activities, they have the right to present the tribunal with opinions on how to rectify them.

Article 113 When the court session opens, the chief judge is to ascertain whether the parties are present in court and announce the subject matter of the case, announce the names of the members of the collegial panel, the court clerk, the public prosecutor, the defender, expert witnesses and interpreters, inform the parties of their right to apply for the withdrawal of members of the collegial panel, the court clerk, the public prosecutor, expert witnesses and interpreters, and inform the defendant of his right to defence.

Article 114 After the public prosecutor has read out the bill of prosecution in the courtroom, the adjudication personnel are to begin to question the defendant.

The public prosecutor may interrogate the defendant with the permission of the chief judge.

After the adjudication personnel have questioned the defendant, the victim, the plaintiff in a supplementary civil action and the defender may put questions to the defendant with the permission of the chief judge.

Article 115 When questioning a witness, the adjudication personnel and public prosecutor shall inform him that he must provide testimony according to the facts and inform him of the legal responsibility he must bear for intentionally giving false testimony or for concealing criminal evidence. Parties and defenders may request the chief judge to put questions to witnesses or expert witnesses or may request permission from the chief judge to put their questions directly. When the chief judge considers that the content of the questioning bears no relation to the case, he shall put a stop to it.

Article 116 The adjudication personnel shall show the material evidence to the defendant and have him identify it. Transcripts of testimony of witnesses who are not present in court, conclusions of the expert evaluations of expert witnesses, transcripts of inspections, and other documents serving as evidence shall be read out in court and the opinions of parties and defenders heard.

Article 117 During the process of the courtroom

hearing, parties and defenders have the right to apply for the notification of new witnesses to come to court for the obtaining of new material evidence and to apply for new expert evaluation or inspection.

The tribunal shall make a decision whether to approve the above applications.

Article 118 After the inquiry by the tribunal, the public prosecutor shall speak, the victim shall speak, and then the defendant shall make his statement and defence, the defender shall conduct the defence, and there may be debate. After the chief judge has announced the closing of debate, the defendant has the right to make a final statement.

Article 119 During the process of the courtroom adjudication, if participants in the proceedings violate order in the courtroom, the chief judge shall warn them to cease; if the circumstances are serious, they may be ordered to leave the courtroom or their criminal responsibility may be investigated according to law.

Article 120 After the defendant makes his final statement, the chief judge is to announce a recess, the collegial panel is to conduct its deliberations, and based on the facts and evidence that have been clarified and on the relevant provisions of law, render a judgment as to whether the defendant is guilty or innocent, what crime he committed, and what criminal punishment is to be applied, or whether he should be exempted from criminal punishment.

Article 121 The announcement of judgment is in all cases to be made in public.

In cases where the judgment is announced at the court session, the written judgment shall be delivered to the parties and the people's procuratorate that initiated the public prosecution within five days; in cases where the judgment is announced on a fixed date, the written judgment shall be delivered to the parties and the people's procuratorate that initiated the public prosecution immediately upon announcement.

Article 122 The written judgment shall be signed by the members of the collegial panel and by the court clerk, and the time limit for appeal and the appellate court are to be clearly stated therein.

Article 123 If during the process of the courtroom adjudication one of the following circumstances that influence the conduct of the adjudication is encountered, the hearing may be postponed:

1. If it becomes necessary to notify new witnesses to come to court, to obtain new material evidence, or to make a new expert evaluation or inspection;

2. If the procuratorial personnel discover that a case for which they initiated a public prosecution requires supplementary investigation, and present a proposal to this effect;

3. If the collegial panel considers that the evidence is incomplete or discovers new facts, requiring it to return the case to the people's procuratorate for supplementary investigation or to make its own inquiry; or

4. If the adjudication cannot be conducted because of a party's application for withdrawal.

Article 124 The court clerk shall make a transcript of all the activities of the courtroom adjudication, to be signed by the chief judge and the court clerk after being checked and approved by the chief judge.

The portion of the courtroom transcript comprising the testimony of witnesses shall be read out in court or delivered to the witnesses to read. After the witnesses acknowledge that it is free of error, they shall sign or place their seals upon it.

The courtroom transcript shall be delivered to the parties to read or shall be read out to them. If the parties consider that there are omissions or errors in the record, they may request supplementation or correction. After the parties have acknowledged that it is free of error, they shall sign or place their seals upon it.

Article 125 In hearing a case of public prosecution, a people's court shall announce judgment within one month after accepting the case, and it may not extend beyond one month and one-half at the latest.*

SECTION 2 CASES OF PRIVATE PROSECUTION

Article 126 After a people's court conducts a review of a case of private prosecution, it may handle the case according to the following circumstances, respectively:

1. If it is a case where the facts of the crime are clear and there is sufficient evidence, a court session shall be opened and the case adjudicated;

2. If the case requires the initiation of a public prosecution by a people's procuratorate, it shall be transferred to the people's procuratorate;

---

* See note to Article 92, *supra*. — *Trans.*

3. In a case of private prosecution where criminal evidence is lacking, if the private prosecutor does not present supplementary evidence and the people's court is also unable to gather the necessary evidence through its inquiry, it shall persuade the private prosecutor to withdraw the private prosecution or order its rejection; or

4. If it is a case where a defendant's act does not constitute a crime, the court shall persuade the private prosecutor to withdraw the private prosecution or order its rejection.

Article 127 A people's court may conduct mediation in a case of private prosecution; before the judgment is announced, a private prosecutor may arrange a settlement on his own with the defendant or may withdraw his private prosecution.

Article 128 During the proceeding, the defendant in a case of private prosecution may raise a counterclaim against the private prosecutor. The provisions relating to private prosecutions apply to counterclaims.

CHAPTER III PROCEDURE OF SECOND INSTANCE

Article 129 Parties or their legal representatives who do not agree with judgments or orders of first instance of the local people's courts at various levels have the right to appeal in writing or orally to the people's court at the next level up. Defenders or close relatives of a defendant may present appeals with the agreement of the defendant.

Parties to supplementary civil actions and their legal representatives may present appeals regarding the supplementary civil action portions of judgments or orders of first instance of the local people's courts at various levels.

No pretext may be used to deprive a defendant of his right to appeal.

Article 130 When local people's procuratorates at various levels consider that a judgment or order of first instance of a people's court at the same level contains actual error, they shall present a protest to the people's court at the next level up.

Article 131 The time limit for an appeal or protest against a judgment is ten days; the time limit for an appeal or protest against an order is five days; time is counted from the day after a written judgment or written order is received.*

Article 132 When parties present an appeal through the people's court that originally adjudicated the case, the people's court that originally adjudicated the case shall, within three days, transfer the appeal petition together with the case file and the evidence to the people's court at the next level up, and at the same time it shall deliver copies of the appeal petition to the people's procuratorate at the same level and to the other parties.

When parties directly present their appeal to the people's court of second instance, the people's court

---

* The procedures of Article 131 have been modified by the Decision of the Standing Committee of the National People's Congress Regarding the Procedure for Rapid Adjudication of Cases Involving Criminal Elements Who Seriously Endanger Public Security. *See* pp. 239-40 below. — *Trans.*

of second instance shall, within three days, deliver the appeal petition to the people's court that originally adjudicated the case for delivery to the people's procuratorate at the same level and to the other parties.

Article 133 Local people's procuratorates at various levels that protest judgments or orders of first instance of the people's courts at the same level shall present the protest document through the people's court that originally adjudicated the case and send a copy of the protest document to the people's procuratorate at the next level up. The people's court that originally adjudicated the case shall transfer the protest document together with the case file and the evidence to the people's court at the next level up and shall deliver copies of the protest document to the parties.

If the people's procuratorate at the higher level considers the protest inappropriate, it may withdraw the protest from the people's court at the same level and notify the people's procuratorate at the lower level.

Article 134 A people's court of second instance shall conduct a complete review of the facts determined and of the law applied in the judgment of first instance, and is not to be limited to the scope of an appeal or protest.

In cases of joint crimes, if only some of the defendants appeal, a review of the entire case shall be conducted and everything handled together.

Article 135 In cases where a people's procuratorate presents a protest or where a people's court of second instance demands that the people's procuratorate send personnel to appear in court, the people's procuratorate at the same level shall send personnel to appear in court. The people's court of second instance must, ten days before opening the court session, notify the people's procuratorate to examine the case file.

Article 136 In a case of appeal or protest against a judgment of first instance, the people's court of second instance shall, after a hearing, handle the case according to the following circumstances, respectively:

1. If the determination of facts and the application of law in the original judgment are correct and the punishment appropriately decided, it shall order rejection of the appeal or protest and affirm the original judgment;

2. If the determination of facts in the original judgment contains no error but there is error in the application of law or the punishment is inappropriately decided, it shall revise the judgment; or

3. If in the original judgment the facts are unclear or the evidence insufficient, it may revise the judgment after clarifying the facts; it may also order quashing of the original judgment and remand the case to the people's court that originally adjudicated it for a new adjudication.

Article 137 In adjudicating a case appealed by a defendant or his legal representative, defender or close relative, a people's court of second instance may not increase a defendant's criminal punishment.

The limitation provided in the preceding paragraph does not apply to a case where a people's procuratorate presents a protest or a private prosecutor presents an appeal.

Article 138 When a people's court of second instance discovers that a people's court of first instance has violated the litigation procedures stipulated by law and that this may have influenced the correctness of the judgment, it shall quash the original judgment and remand the case to the people's court that originally adjudicated it for a new adjudication.

Article 139 The people's court that originally adjudicated a case shall conduct the adjudication of a case remanded to it for new adjudication in accordance with the procedure of first instance. The parties may appeal and the people's procuratorate at the same level may protest the judgment rendered after the new adjudication.

Article 140 After reviewing an appeal or protest against an order of first instance, a people's court of second instance shall order rejection of the appeal or protest, or quashing or revision of the original order, in accordance with the respective circumstances and with reference to the stipulations of Articles 136, 138 and 139 of this Law.

Article 141 Except where this Chapter has made other provisions, the procedure for adjudication by a people's court of second instance of cases of appeal or protest is to be conducted with reference to the stipulations on the procedure of first instance.

Article 142 The people's courts of second instance shall conclude adjudication within one month after receiving a case of appeal or protest, and it may not extend beyond one month and one-half at the latest,*

---

* See note to Article 92, *supra*. — *Trans.*

Article 143 The judgments and orders of second instance and the judgments and orders of the Supreme People's Court are all judgments and orders of final instance.

CHAPTER IV PROCEDURE FOR REVIEW OF DEATH SENTENCES

Article 144 Sentences of death are to be approved by the Supreme People's Court.

Article 145 Cases of first instance where an intermediate people's court imposes a sentence of death and the defendant does not appeal shall be submitted to the Supreme People's Court for approval after review by a high people's court. When a high people's court does not agree with a sentence of death, it may bring the case up and adjudicate it or remand it for new adjudication.

Cases of first instance where a high people's court imposes a sentence of death and the defendant does not appeal and cases where a sentence of death is imposed in the second instance shall all be submitted to the Supreme People's Court for approval.*

Article 146 Cases where an intermediate people's court imposes a sentence of death with a two-year suspension of execution are to be approved by a high people's court.

---

* The procedures of Articles 144 and 145 have been modified by the Decision of the Standing Committee of the National People's Congress Regarding the Question of Approval of Cases Involving Death Sentences. *See* pp. 217-18 below. —*Trans.*

Article 147 The review of cases involving sentences of death by the Supreme People's Court and the review of cases involving sentences of death with suspension of execution by a high people's court shall be conducted by a collegial panel composed of three judges.

CHAPTER V PROCEDURE FOR ADJUDICATION SUPERVISION

Article 148 Parties, victims and their family members or other citizens may present petitions regarding judgments or orders that have already become legally effective to the people's courts or the people's procuratorates, but the execution of such judgments or orders cannot be suspended.

Article 149 If presidents of the people's courts at various levels discover that the determination of facts or application of law in judgments and orders of their court that have become legally effective contain actual error, they must send the case to the adjudication committee to be handled.

If the Supreme People's Court discovers that judgments and orders of the people's courts at various levels that have already become legally effective contain actual error or if the people's courts at higher levels discover the same to be true of judgments and orders of the people's courts at lower levels that have already become legally effective, they have the right to bring the cases up and adjudicate them or to direct the people's courts at lower levels to readjudicate them.

If the Supreme People's Procuratorate discovers that judgments and orders of the people's courts at various levels that have already become legally effective contain actual error or if the people's procuratorates at higher levels discover the same to be true of judgments and orders of the people's courts at lower levels that have already become legally effective, they have the right to present a protest in accordance with the procedure of adjudication supervision.

Article 150 A new collegial panel shall be formed for the new adjudication of cases by the people's courts in accordance with the procedure of adjudication supervision. If the case was originally one of first instance, the adjudication shall be conducted according to the procedure of first instance, and the judgment or order made may be appealed or protested; if the case was originally one of second instance or was a case that a people's court at a higher level brought up and adjudicated, the adjudication shall be conducted according to the procedure of second instance and the judgment or order made is to be final.

PART IV   EXECUTION OF SENTENCES

Article 151   Judgments and orders are to be executed after they become legally effective.

The following judgments and orders are judgments and orders that have become legally effective:

1. Judgments and orders where there has been no appeal or protest and where the legally prescribed time limit has already expired;
2. Judgments and orders of final instance; and
3. Judgments of the death penalty approved by the Supreme People's Court and judgments of the death penalty with a two-year suspension of execution approved by the high people's courts.

Article 152   In cases where the people's courts of first instance judge a defendant innocent or exempt from criminal punishment, if the defendant is held in custody, he shall be released immediately after announcement of the judgment.

Article 153   For judgments of the death penalty with immediate execution imposed or approved by the Supreme People's Court, the President of the Supreme People's Court shall sign and issue an order to execute the sentence of death.

Where a criminal sentenced to death with a two-year suspension of execution truly repents or demonstrates meritorious service during the period of suspension of execution of the sentence of death and should be granted a reduction of sentence according to law, the executing organ is to present a written opinion and submit it to the high people's court in the locality for an order; if there is verified evidence that he has resisted reform in an odious manner and his sentence of death should be executed, the high people's court must submit the matter to the Supreme People's Court for approval.

Article 154 After receiving an order to execute the sentence of death from the Supreme People's Court, the people's courts at lower levels shall, within seven days, deliver the criminal for execution of the sentence. However, if one of the following circumstances is discovered, the execution of the sentence shall be suspended and the matter immediately reported to the Supreme People's Court, and an order made by the Supreme People's Court:

1. If before the execution of the sentence it is discovered that the judgment may contain error; or
2. If the criminal is pregnant.

After elimination of the first reason in the preceding paragraph for suspension of execution of sentence, before the sentence may be executed the matter must be submitted to the President of the Supreme People's Court for him again to sign and issue an order to execute the sentence of death; in cases where the execution of the sentence is suspended for the second reason in the preceding paragraph, the matter shall be submitted to the Supreme People's Court for revision of the judgment according to law.

Article 155 Before a people's court delivers a criminal for execution of the sentence of death, it shall notify the people's procuratorate at the same level to send personnel to be present at the scene to supervise.

The adjudication personnel directing the execution of the sentence shall verify the identity of the criminal, ask if he has last words or letters, and then deliver him to the execution personnel for execution of the sentence of death. Before the execution of the sentence, if it is discovered that there may be error, the execution of the sentence shall be suspended and the matter submitted to the Supreme People's Court for an order.

Execution of sentences of death shall be publicly announced but shall not take place in public view.

After execution of the death sentence the court clerk on the scene shall make a transcript of it. The people's court that delivered the criminal for execution of the sentence shall report the circumstances of the execution of the sentence of death to the Supreme People's Court.

After execution of the sentence of death, the people's court that delivered the criminal for execution of the sentence shall notify the family of the criminal.

Article 156 In cases of criminals sentenced to death with a two-year suspension of execution, to life imprisonment, fixed-term imprisonment or criminal detention, the people's court delivering the criminal for execution of the sentence shall deliver the notice of execution of the sentence and the written judgment to the prison or other place of reform through labour for execution of the sentence, and the executing organ is to inform the family of the criminal.

Criminals sentenced to fixed-term imprisonment or criminal detention shall, upon completion of the execution of their sentence, be issued a certificate of completion of sentence and release by the executing organ.

Article 157 Criminals sentenced to life imprisonment, fixed-term imprisonment or criminal detention may, in one of the following circumstances, have their sentence temporarily executed outside of prison:

1. If a criminal has a serious illness and needs to remain out of custody and obtain medical treatment; or

2. If the criminal is a woman who is pregnant or is nursing her own baby.

In cases where a criminal's sentence is to be executed outside of prison, the public security organs may entrust the public security station at the criminal's original place of residence with the execution of the sentence, and basic-level organizations or the original unit of the criminal are to assist in conducting supervision.

Article 158 A criminal who has been sentenced to a suspended fixed-term of imprisonment is to be turned over by the public security organs to his unit or to a basic-level organization for observation.

A criminal who has been paroled, during the probation period for parole, is to be supervised by the public security organs.

Article 159 Sentences of criminals sentenced to control or deprivation of political rights are to be executed by the public security organs. Upon completion of the execution of the sentence, the executing organs shall notify the criminal himself and publicly announce to the masses concerned the ending of control or the restoration of political rights.

Article 160 In cases where a criminal has been sentenced to pay a fine but has not paid by the expiration of the time limit, the people's court shall compel him to pay; in the case of a person who has true difficulties in paying because he has suffered irresistible calamity, an order may be made to reduce the fine or exempt him from payment.

Article 161 All judgments of confiscation of property, regardless of whether applied in a supplementary or independent manner, are to be executed by the people's courts, which may, when necessary, collaborate with the public security organs in executing such judgments.

Article 162 In cases where a criminal commits further crimes during the period in which he is serving his sentence, or where criminal conduct is discovered that was not discovered at the time of judgment, prisons and reform-through-labour organs shall transfer the matter to the people's procuratorate for handling.

When a criminal sentenced to control, criminal detention, fixed-term imprisonment or life imprisonment truly repents or demonstrates meritorious service during the period of execution of his sentence and should be granted a reduction of sentence or parole according to law, the executing organ is to submit a written opinion to the people's court for consideration and an order.

Article 163 If, while executing punishment, prisons and reform through labour organs consider a judgment mistaken, or if the criminal presents a petition, the matter shall be referred for handling to the people's procuratorate or the people's court that made the original judgment.

Article 164 The people's procuratorates are to exercise supervision to determine whether or not the execution of judgments or orders in criminal cases and the activities of prisons, detention houses and reform-through-labour organs are lawful. If they discover any illegalities, they shall notify the executing organ to rectify them.

中华人民共和国刑事诉讼法

(一九七九年七月一日第五届全国
人民代表大会第二次会议通过,
自一九八〇年一月一日起施行)

目 录

第一编 总 则·······173
- 第一章 指导思想、任务和基本原则···173
- 第二章 管辖···176
- 第三章 回避···178
- 第四章 辩护···179
- 第五章 证据···180
- 第六章 强制措施···181
- 第七章 附带民事诉讼···185
- 第八章 期间、送达···186
- 第九章 其他规定···187

第二编 立案、侦查和提起公诉···188
- 第一章 立案···188
- 第二章 侦查···189
  - 第一节 讯问被告人···189
  - 第二节 询问证人···190
  - 第三节 勘验、检查···191
  - 第四节 搜查···192
  - 第五节 扣押物证、书证···193
  - 第六节 鉴定···194
  - 第七节 通缉···194
  - 第八节 侦查终结···195
- 第三章 提起公诉···195

第三编 审 判···198

第一章　审判组织……………………………………………198
第二章　第一审程序…………………………………………199
　第一节　公诉案件…………………………………………199
　第二节　自诉案件…………………………………………204
第三章　第二审程序…………………………………………205
第四章　死刑复核程序………………………………………208
第五章　审判监督程序………………………………………209

第四编　执　　行……………………………………………211

第一编 总 则

第一章 指导思想、任务和基本原则

第一条 中华人民共和国刑事诉讼法,以马克思列宁主义毛泽东思想为指针,以宪法为根据,结合我国各族人民实行无产阶级领导的、工农联盟为基础的人民民主专政即无产阶级专政的具体经验和打击敌人、保护人民的实际需要制定。

第二条 中华人民共和国刑事诉讼法的任务,是保证准确、及时地查明犯罪事实,正确应用法律,惩罚犯罪分子,保障无罪的人不受刑事追究,教育公民自觉遵守法律,积极同犯罪行为作斗争,以维护社会主义法制,保护公民的人身权利、民主权利和其他权利,保障社会主义革命和社会主义建设事业的顺利进行。

第三条 对刑事案件的侦查、拘留、预审,由公安机关负责。批准逮捕和检察(包括侦查)、提起公诉,由人民检察院负责。审判由人民法院负责。其他任何机关、团体和个人都无权行使这些权力。

人民法院、人民检察院和公安机关进行刑事诉讼，必须严格遵守本法和其他法律的有关规定。

第四条 人民法院、人民检察院和公安机关进行刑事诉讼，必须依靠群众，必须以事实为根据，以法律为准绳。对于一切公民，在适用法律上一律平等，在法律面前，不允许有任何特权。

第五条 人民法院、人民检察院和公安机关进行刑事诉讼，应当分工负责，互相配合，互相制约，以保证准确有效地执行法律。

第六条 各民族公民都有用本民族语言文字进行诉讼的权利。人民法院、人民检察院和公安机关对于不通晓当地通用的语言文字的诉讼参与人，应当为他们翻译。

在少数民族聚居或者多民族杂居的地区，应当用当地通用的语言进行审讯，用当地通用的文字发布判决书、布告和其他文件。

第七条 人民法院审判案件，实行两审终审制。

第八条 人民法院审判案件，除本法另有规定的以外，一律公开进行。被告人有权获得辩护，人民法院有义务保证被告人获得辩护。

第九条 人民法院审判案件，依照本法实行人民陪审员陪审的制度。

第十条 人民法院、人民检察院和公安机关应当保障诉讼参与人依法享有的诉讼权利。

对于不满十八岁的未成年人犯罪的案件，在讯问和审判时，可以通知被告人的法定代理人到场。

诉讼参与人对于审判人员、检察人员和侦查人员侵犯公民诉讼权利和人身侮辱的行为，有权提出控告。

第十一条 有下列情形之一的，不追究刑事责任，已经追究的，应当撤销案件，或者不起诉，或者宣告无罪：

（一）情节显著轻微、危害不大，不认为是犯罪的；

（二）犯罪已过追诉时效期限的；

（三）经特赦令免除刑罚的；

（四）依照刑法告诉才处理的犯罪，没有告诉或者撤回告诉的；

（五）被告人死亡的；

（六）其他法律、法令规定免予追究刑事责任的。

第十二条 对于外国人犯罪应当追究刑事责任的，适用本法的规定。

对于享有外交特权和豁免权的外国人犯罪应当追究刑事责任的,通过外交途径解决。

第二章 管 辖

第十三条 告诉才处理和其他不需要进行侦查的轻微的刑事案件,由人民法院直接受理,并可以进行调解。

贪污罪、侵犯公民民主权利罪、渎职罪以及人民检察院认为需要自己直接受理的其他案件,由人民检察院立案侦查和决定是否提起公诉。

第一、二款规定以外的其他案件的侦查,都由公安机关进行。

第十四条 基层人民法院管辖第一审普通刑事案件,但是依照本法由上级人民法院管辖的除外。

第十五条 中级人民法院管辖下列第一审刑事案件:

(一)反革命案件;

(二)判处无期徒刑、死刑的普通刑事案件;

(三)外国人犯罪或者我国公民侵犯外国人合法权利的刑事案件。

第十六条　高级人民法院管辖的第一审刑事案件,是全省(直辖市、自治区)性的重大刑事案件。

第十七条　最高人民法院管辖的第一审刑事案件,是全国性的重大刑事案件。

第十八条　上级人民法院在必要的时候,可以审判下级人民法院管辖的第一审刑事案件,也可以把自己管辖的第一审刑事案件交由下级人民法院审判;下级人民法院认为案情重大、复杂需要由上级人民法院审判的第一审刑事案件,可以请求移送上一级人民法院审判。

第十九条　刑事案件由犯罪地的人民法院管辖。如果由被告人居住地的人民法院审判更为适宜的,可以由被告人居住地的人民法院管辖。

第二十条　几个同级人民法院都有权管辖的案件,由最初受理的人民法院审判。在必要的时候,可以移送主要犯罪地的人民法院审判。

第二十一条　上级人民法院可以指定下级人民法院审判管辖不明的案件,也可以指定下级人民法院将案件移送其他人民法院审判。

第二十二条　专门人民法院案件的管辖另行规定。

第三章 回 避

第二十三条 审判人员、检察人员、侦查人员有下列情形之一的,应当自行回避,当事人及其法定代理人也有权要求他们回避:

(一)是本案的当事人或者是当事人的近亲属的;

(二)本人或者他的近亲属和本案有利害关系的;

(三)担任过本案的证人、鉴定人、辩护人或者附带民事诉讼当事人的代理人的;

(四)与本案当事人有其他关系,可能影响公正处理案件的。

第二十四条 审判人员、检察人员、侦查人员的回避,应当分别由院长、检察长、公安机关负责人决定;院长的回避,由本院审判委员会决定;检察长和公安机关负责人的回避,由同级人民检察院检察委员会决定。

对侦查人员的回避作出决定前,侦查人员不能停止对案件的侦查。

对驳回申请回避的决定,当事人可以申请复议一次。

第二十五条 本法第二十三条、第二十四条的规定也适用于书记员、翻译人员和鉴定人。

第四章 辩　　护

第二十六条 被告人除自己行使辩护权以外，还可以委托下列的人辩护：

（一）律师；

（二）人民团体或者被告人所在单位推荐的，或者经人民法院许可的公民；

（三）被告人的近亲属、监护人。

第二十七条 公诉人出庭公诉的案件，被告人没有委托辩护人的，人民法院可以为他指定辩护人。

被告人是聋、哑或者未成年人而没有委托辩护人的，人民法院应当为他指定辩护人。

第二十八条 辩护人的责任是根据事实和法律，提出证明被告人无罪、罪轻或者减轻、免除其刑事责任的材料和意见，维护被告人的合法权益。

第二十九条 辩护律师可以查阅本案材料，了解案情，可以同在押的被告人会见和通信；其他的辩护人经过人民法院许可，也可以了解案情，同在押的被告人会见和通信。

第三十条 在审判过程中，被告人可以拒绝辩护人继续为他辩护，也可以另行委托辩护人辩护。

第五章 证 据

第三十一条 证明案件真实情况的一切事实，都是证据。

证据有下列六种：

（一）物证、书证；

（二）证人证言；

（三）被害人陈述；

（四）被告人供述和辩解；

（五）鉴定结论；

（六）勘验、检查笔录。

以上证据必须经过查证属实，才能作为定案的根据。

第三十二条 审判人员、检察人员、侦查人员必须依照法定程序，收集能够证实被告人有罪或者无罪、犯罪情节轻重的各种证据。严禁刑讯逼供和以威胁、引诱、欺骗以及其他非法的方法收集证据。必须保证一切与案件有关或者了解案情的公民，有客观地充分地提供证据的条件，除特殊情况外，并且可以吸收他们协助调查。

第三十三条 公安机关提请批准逮捕书、人民检察院起诉书、人民法院判决书，必须忠实于事实真象。故意隐瞒事实真象的，应当追究责任。

第三十四条 人民法院、人民检察院和公安机关有权向有关的国家机关、企业、事业单位、人民公社、人民团体和公民收集、调取证据。

对于涉及国家机密的证据,应当保密。

凡是伪造证据、隐匿证据或者毁灭证据的,无论属于何方,必须受法律追究。

第三十五条 对一切案件的判处都要重证据,重调查研究,不轻信口供。只有被告人供述,没有其他证据的,不能认定被告人有罪和处以刑罚;没有被告人供述,证据充分确实的,可以认定被告人有罪和处以刑罚。

第三十六条 证人证言必须在法庭上经过公诉人、被害人和被告人、辩护人双方讯问、质证,听取各方证人的证言并经过查实以后,才能作为定案的根据。法庭查明证人有意作伪证或者隐匿罪证时,应当依法处理。

第三十七条 凡是知道案件情况的人,都有作证的义务。

生理上、精神上有缺陷或者年幼,不能辨别是非、不能正确表达的人,不能作证人。

第六章 强制措施

第三十八条 人民法院、人民检察院和公安

机关根据案件情况,对被告人可以拘传、取保候审或者监视居住。

被监视居住的被告人不得离开指定的区域。监视居住由当地公安派出所执行,或者由受委托的人民公社、被告人的所在单位执行。

对被告人采取取保候审、监视居住的,如果情况发生变化,应当撤销或者变更。

第三十九条 逮捕人犯,必须经过人民检察院批准或者人民法院决定,由公安机关执行。

第四十条 对主要犯罪事实已经查清,可能判处徒刑以上刑罚的人犯,采取取保候审、监视居住等方法,尚不足以防止发生社会危险性,而有逮捕必要的,应即依法逮捕。

对应当逮捕的人犯,如果患有严重疾病,或者是正在怀孕、哺乳自己婴儿的妇女,可以采用取保候审或者监视居住的办法。

第四十一条 公安机关对于罪该逮捕的现行犯或者重大嫌疑分子,如果有下列情形之一的,可以先行拘留:

(一)正在预备犯罪、实行犯罪或者在犯罪后即时被发觉的;

(二)被害人或者在场亲眼看见的人指认他犯罪的;

(三)在身边或者住处发现有犯罪证据的;

（四）犯罪后企图自杀、逃跑或者在逃的；

（五）有毁灭、伪造证据或者串供可能的；

（六）身份不明有流窜作案重大嫌疑的；

（七）正在进行"打砸抢"和严重破坏工作、生产、社会秩序的。

第四十二条　对于下列人犯，任何公民都可以立即扭送公安机关、人民检察院或者人民法院处理：

（一）正在实行犯罪或者在犯罪后即时被发觉的；

（二）通缉在案的；

（三）越狱逃跑的；

（四）正在被追捕的。

第四十三条　公安机关拘留人的时候，必须出示拘留证。

拘留后，除有碍侦查或者无法通知的情形以外，应当把拘留的原因和羁押的处所，在二十四小时以内，通知被拘留人的家属或者他的所在单位。

第四十四条　公安机关对于被拘留的人，应当在拘留后的二十四小时以内进行讯问。在发现不应当拘留的时候，必须立即释放，发给释放证明。对需要逮捕而证据还不充足的，可以取保候审或者监视居住。

第四十五条 公安机关要求逮捕人犯的时候,应当写出提请批准逮捕书,连同案卷材料、证据,一并移送同级人民检察院审查批准。必要时,人民检察院可以派人参加公安机关对于重大案件的讨论。

第四十六条 人民检察院审查批准逮捕人犯由检察长决定。重大案件应当提交检察委员会讨论决定。

第四十七条 人民检察院对于公安机关提请批准逮捕的案件进行审查后,应当根据情况分别作出批准逮捕,不批准逮捕或者补充侦查的决定。

第四十八条 公安机关对被拘留的人,认为需要逮捕的,应当在拘留后的三日以内,提请人民检察院审查批准。在特殊情况下,提请审查批准的时间可以延长一日至四日。人民检察院应当在接到公安机关提请批准逮捕书后的三日以内,作出批准逮捕或者不批准逮捕的决定。人民检察院不批准逮捕的,公安机关应当在接到通知后立即释放,发给释放证明。

公安机关或者人民检察院如果没有按照前款规定办理,被拘留的人或者他的家属有权要求释放,公安机关或者人民检察院应当立即释放。

第四十九条 公安机关对人民检察院不批准

逮捕的决定，认为有错误的时候，可以要求复议，但是必须将被拘留的人立即释放。如果意见不被接受，可以向上一级人民检察院提请复核。上级人民检察院应当立即复核，作出是否变更的决定，通知下级人民检察院和公安机关执行。

第五十条　公安机关逮捕人的时候，必须出示逮捕证。

逮捕后，除有碍侦查或者无法通知的情形以外，应当把逮捕的原因和羁押的处所，在二十四小时以内通知被逮捕人的家属或者他的所在单位。

第五十一条　人民法院、人民检察院对于各自决定逮捕的人，公安机关对于经人民检察院批准逮捕的人，都必须在逮捕后的二十四小时以内进行讯问。在发现不应当逮捕的时候，必须立即释放，发给释放证明。

第五十二条　人民检察院在审查批准逮捕工作中，如果发现公安机关的侦查活动有违法情况，应当通知公安机关予以纠正，公安机关应当将纠正情况通知人民检察院。

第七章　附带民事诉讼

第五十三条　被害人由于被告人的犯罪行为

而遭受物质损失的,在刑事诉讼过程中,有权提起附带民事诉讼。

如果是国家财产、集体财产遭受损失的,人民检察院在提起公诉的时候,可以提起附带民事诉讼。

人民法院在必要的时候,可以查封或者扣押被告人的财产。

第五十四条 附带民事诉讼应当同刑事案件一并审判,只有为了防止刑事案件审判的过分迟延,才可以在刑事案件审判后,由同一审判组织继续审理附带民事诉讼。

第八章 期间、送达

第五十五条 期间以时、日、月计算。

期间开始的时和日不算在期间以内。

法定期间不包括路途上的时间。上诉状或者其他文件在期满前已经交邮的,不算过期。

第五十六条 当事人由于不能抗拒的原因或者有其他正当理由而耽误期限的,在障碍消除后五日以内,可以申请继续进行应当在期满以前完成的诉讼活动。

前款申请是否准许,由人民法院裁定。

第五十七条 送达传票、通知书和其他诉讼

文件应当交给收件人本人；如果本人不在，可以交给他的成年家属或者所在单位的负责人员代收。

收件人本人或者代收人拒绝接收或者拒绝签名、盖章的时候，送达人可以邀请他的邻居或者其他见证人到场，说明情况，把文件留在他的住处，在送达证上记明拒绝的事由、送达的日期，由送达人签名，即认为已经送达。

第九章 其他规定

第五十八条 本法下列用语的含意是：

（一）侦查是指公安机关、人民检察院在办理案件过程中，依照法律进行的专门调查工作和有关的强制性措施；

（二）"当事人"是指自诉人、被告人、附带民事诉讼的原告人和被告人；

（三）"法定代理人"是指被代理人的父母、养父母、监护人和负有保护责任的机关、团体的代表；

（四）"诉讼参与人"是指当事人、被害人、法定代理人、辩护人、证人、鉴定人和翻译人员；

（五）"近亲属"是指夫、妻、父、母、子、女、同胞兄弟姊妹。

第二编 立案、侦查和提起公诉

第一章 立 案

第五十九条 机关、团体、企业、事业单位和公民发现有犯罪事实或者犯罪嫌疑人，有权利也有义务按照本法第十三条规定的管辖范围，向公安机关、人民检察院或者人民法院提出控告和检举。

公安机关、人民检察院或者人民法院对于控告、检举和犯罪人的自首，都应当接受。对于不属于自己管辖的，应当移送主管机关处理，并且通知控告人、检举人；对于不属于自己管辖而又必须采取紧急措施的，应当先采取紧急措施，然后移送主管机关。

第六十条 控告、检举可以用书面或者口头提出。接受口头控告、检举的工作人员，应当写成笔录，经宣读无误后，由控告人、检举人签名或者盖章。

接受控告、检举的工作人员，应当向控告人、检举人说明诬告应负的法律责任。但是，只要不是捏造事实，伪造证据，即使控告、检举的事实有出入，甚至是错告的，也要和诬告严格加以区别。

控告人、检举人如果不愿公开自己的姓名，在侦查期间，应当为他保守秘密。

第六十一条 人民法院、人民检察院或者公安机关对于控告、检举和自首的材料，应当按照管辖范围，迅速进行审查，认为有犯罪事实需要追究刑事责任的时候，应当立案；认为没有犯罪事实，或者犯罪事实显著轻微，不需要追究刑事责任的时候，不予立案，并且将不立案的原因通知控告人。控告人如果不服，可以申请复议。

第二章 侦 查

第一节 讯问被告人

第六十二条 讯问被告人必须由人民检察院或者公安机关的侦查人员负责进行。讯问的时候，侦查人员不得少于二人。

第六十三条 对于不需要逮捕、拘留的被告人，可以传唤到指定的地点或者到他的住处、所在单位进行讯问，但是应当出示人民检察院或者公安机关的证明文件。

第六十四条 侦查人员在讯问被告人的时

候,应当首先讯问被告人是否有犯罪行为,让他陈述有罪的情节或者无罪的辩解,然后向他提出问题。被告人对侦查人员的提问,应当如实回答。但是对与本案无关的问题,有拒绝回答的权利。

第六十五条 讯问聋、哑的被告人,应当有通晓聋、哑手势的人参加,并且将这种情况记明笔录。

第六十六条 讯问笔录应当交被告人核对,对于没有阅读能力的,应当向他宣读。如果记载有遗漏或者差错,被告人可以提出补充或者改正。被告人承认笔录没有错误后,应当签名或者盖章。侦查人员也应当在笔录上签名。被告人请求自行书写供述的,应当准许。必要的时候,侦查人员也可以要被告人亲笔书写供词。

第二节 询问证人

第六十七条 侦查人员询问证人,可以到证人的所在单位或者住处进行,但是必须出示人民检察院或者公安机关的证明文件。在必要的时候,也可以通知证人到人民检察院或者公安机关提供证言。

询问证人应当个别进行。

第六十八条 询问证人,应当告知他应当如

实地提供证据、证言和有意作伪证或者隐匿罪证要负的法律责任。

第六十九条 本法第六十六条的规定，也适用于询问证人。

第七十条 询问被害人，适用本节各条规定。

第三节 勘验、检查

第七十一条 侦查人员对于与犯罪有关的场所、物品、人身、尸体应当进行勘验或者检查。在必要的时候，可以指派或者聘请具有专门知识的人，在侦查人员的主持下进行勘验、检查。

第七十二条 任何单位和个人，都有义务保护犯罪现场，并且立即通知公安机关派员勘验。

第七十三条 侦查人员执行勘验、检查，必须持有公安机关的证明文件。

第七十四条 对于死因不明的尸体，公安机关有权决定解剖，并通知死者家属到场。

第七十五条 为了确定被害人、被告人的某些特征、伤害情况或者生理状态，可以对人身进行检查。

被告人如果拒绝检查，侦查人员认为必要的时候，可以强制检查。

检查妇女的身体，应当由女工作人员或者医

师进行。

第七十六条 勘验、检查的情况应当写成笔录,由参加勘验、检查的人和见证人签名或者盖章。

第七十七条 人民检察院审查案件时,对公安机关的勘验、检查,认为需要复验、复查时,可以要求公安机关复验、复查,并且可以派检察人员参加。

第七十八条 为了查明案情,在必要的时候,经公安局长批准,可以进行侦查实验。

侦查实验,禁止一切足以造成危险、侮辱人格或者有伤风化的行为。

第四节 搜 查

第七十九条 为了收集犯罪证据、查获犯罪人,侦查人员可以对被告人以及可能隐藏罪犯或者犯罪证据的人的身体、物品、住处和其他有关的地方进行搜查。

第八十条 任何单位和个人,有义务按照人民检察院和公安机关的要求,交出可以证明被告人有罪或者无罪的物证、书证。

第八十一条 进行搜查,必须向被搜查人出示搜查证。

在执行逮捕、拘留的时候,遇有紧急情况,

中华人民共和国刑事诉讼法

不另用搜查证也可以进行搜查。

第八十二条 在搜查的时候,应当有被搜查人或者他的家属,邻居或者其他见证人在场。

搜查妇女的身体,应当由女工作人员进行。

第八十三条 搜查的情况应当写成笔录,由侦查人员和被搜查人或者他的家属,邻居或者其他见证人签名或者盖章。如果被搜查人或者他的家属在逃或者拒绝签名、盖章,应当在笔录上注明。

第五节 扣押物证、书证

第八十四条 在勘验、搜查中发现的可用以证明被告人有罪或者无罪的各种物品和文件,应当扣押;与案件无关的物品、文件,不得扣押。

对于扣押的物品、文件,要妥善保管或者封存,不得使用或者损毁。

第八十五条 对于扣押的物品和文件,应当会同在场见证人和被扣押物品持有人查点清楚,当场开列清单一式二份,由侦查人员、见证人和持有人签名或者盖章,一份交给持有人,另一份附卷备查。

第八十六条 侦查人员认为需要扣押被告人的邮件、电报的时候,经公安机关或者人民检察院批准,即可通知邮电机关将有关的邮件、电报检交扣押。

不需要继续扣押的时候,应即通知邮电机关。

第八十七条 对于扣押的物品、文件、邮件、电报,经查明确实与案件无关的,应当迅速退还原主或者原邮电机关。

第六节 鉴 定

第八十八条 为了查明案情,需要解决案件中某些专门性问题的时候,应当指派、聘请有专门知识的人进行鉴定。

第八十九条 鉴定人进行鉴定后,应当写出鉴定结论,并签名。

第九十条 用作证据的鉴定结论应当告知被告人。如果被告人提出申请,可以补充鉴定或者重新鉴定。

第七节 通 缉

第九十一条 应当逮捕的被告人如果在逃,公安机关可以发布通缉令,采取有效措施,追捕归案。

各级公安机关在自己管辖的地区以内,可以直接发布通缉令;超出自己管辖的地区,应当报请有权决定的上级机关发布。

第八节 侦查终结

第九十二条 对被告人在侦查中的羁押期限不得超过二个月。案情复杂、期限届满不能终结的案件，可以经上一级人民检察院批准延长一个月。

特别重大、复杂的案件，依照前款规定延长后仍不能终结的，由最高人民检察院报请全国人民代表大会常务委员会批准延期审理。

第九十三条 人民检察院侦查的案件，侦查终结后，应当作出提起公诉、免予起诉或者撤销案件的决定。

公安机关侦查的案件，侦查终结后，应当写出起诉意见书或者免予起诉意见书，连同案卷材料、证据一并移送同级人民检察院审查决定。

第九十四条 在侦查过程中，发现不应对被告人追究刑事责任的，应当撤销案件；被告人已被逮捕的，应当立即释放，发给释放证明，并且通知原批准逮捕的人民检察院。

第三章 提起公诉

第九十五条 凡需要提起公诉或者免予起诉的案件，一律由人民检察院审查决定。

第九十六条 人民检察院审查案件的时候，

必须查明:

(一)犯罪事实、情节是否清楚,证据是否确实、充分,犯罪性质和罪名的认定是否正确;

(二)有无遗漏罪行和其他应当追究刑事责任的人;

(三)是否属于不应追究刑事责任的;

(四)有无附带民事诉讼;

(五)侦查活动是否合法。

第九十七条 人民检察院对于公安机关移送起诉或者免予起诉的案件,应当在一个月以内作出决定,重大、复杂的案件,可以延长半个月。

第九十八条 人民检察院审查案件,应当讯问被告人。

第九十九条 人民检察院审查案件,对于需要补充侦查的,可以自行侦查,也可以退回公安机关补充侦查。

对于补充侦查的案件,应当在一个月以内补充侦查完毕。

第一百条 人民检察院认为被告人的犯罪事实已经查清,证据确实、充分,依法应当追究刑事责任的,应当作出起诉决定,按照审判管辖的规定,向人民法院提起公诉。

第一百零一条 依照刑法规定不需要判处刑

罚或者免除刑罚的，人民检察院可以免予起诉。

第一百零二条 免予起诉的决定，应当公开宣布，并且将免予起诉决定书交给被告人和他的所在单位。如果被告人在押，应当立即释放。

对于公安机关移送起诉的案件，人民检察院决定免予起诉的，应当将免予起诉决定书送公安机关。公安机关认为免予起诉的决定有错误的时候，可以要求复议，如果意见不被接受，可以向上一级人民检察院提请复核。

对于有被害人的案件，决定免予起诉的，人民检察院应当将免予起诉决定书送被害人。被害人如果不服，可以在收到后七日内向人民检察院申诉。人民检察院应当将复查结果告知被害人。

第一百零三条 对于免予起诉的决定，被告人如果不服，可以在七日内向人民检察院申诉。人民检察院应当作出复查决定，通知被告人，同时抄送公安机关。

第一百零四条 被告人有本法第十一条规定的情形之一的，人民检察院应当作出不起诉决定。

本法第一百零二条的规定适用于不起诉的决定。

第三编 审 判

第一章 审判组识

第一百零五条 基层人民法院、中级人民法院审判第一审案件，除自诉案件和其他轻微的刑事案件可以由审判员一人独任审判以外，应当由审判员一人、人民陪审员二人组成合议庭进行。

高级人民法院、最高人民法院审判第一审案件，应当由审判员一人至三人、人民陪审员二人至四人组成合议庭进行。

人民陪审员在人民法院执行职务，同审判员有同等的权利。

人民法院审判上诉和抗诉案件，由审判员三人至五人组成合议庭进行。

合议庭由院长或者庭长指定审判员一人担任审判长。院长或者庭长参加审判案件的时候，自己担任审判长。

第一百零六条 合议庭进行评议的时候，如果意见分歧，应当少数服从多数，但是少数人的意见应当写入笔录。评议笔录由合议庭的组成人员签名。

第一百零七条 凡是重大的或者疑难的案件，院长认为需要提交审判委员会讨论的，由院长提交审判委员会讨论决定。审判委员会的决定，合议庭应当执行。

第二章　第一审程序

第一节　公诉案件

第一百零八条 人民法院对提起公诉的案件进行审查后，对于犯罪事实清楚、证据充分的，应当决定开庭审判；对于主要事实不清、证据不足的，可以退回人民检察院补充侦查；对于不需要判刑的，可以要求人民检察院撤回起诉。

第一百零九条 人民法院在必要的时候，可以进行勘验、检查、搜查、扣押和鉴定。

第一百一十条 人民法院决定开庭审判后，应当进行下列工作：

（一）确定合议庭的组成人员；

（二）将人民检察院的起诉书副本至迟在开庭七日以前送达被告人，并且告知被告人可以委托辩护人，或者在必要时为被告人指定辩护人；

（三）将开庭的时间、地点在开庭三日以前通知人民检察院；

（四）传唤当事人，通知辩护人、证人、鉴定人和翻译人员，传票和通知书至迟在开庭三日以前送达；

（五）公开审判的案件，先期公布案由、被告人姓名、开庭时间和地点。

上述活动情形应当写入笔录，由审判人员和书记员签名。

第一百一十一条　人民法院审判第一审案件应当公开进行。但是有关国家机密或者个人阴私的案件，不公开审理。

十四岁以上不满十六岁未成年人犯罪的案件，一律不公开审理。十六岁以上不满十八岁未成年人犯罪的案件，一般也不公开审理。

对于不公开审理的案件，应当当庭宣布不公开审理的理由。

第一百一十二条　人民法院审判公诉案件，除罪行较轻经人民法院同意的以外，人民检察院应当派员出席法庭支持公诉。

出庭的检察人员发现审判活动有违法情况，有权向法庭提出纠正意见。

第一百一十三条　开庭时，审判长查明当事人是否到庭，宣布案由；宣布合议庭的组成人员、书记员、公诉人、辩护人、鉴定人和翻译人员的名单；告知当事人有权对合议庭组成人员、书记员、公诉人、鉴定人和翻译人员申请回避；告知被告人享有辩护权利。

第一百一十四条 公诉人在审判庭上宣读起诉书后，审判人员开始审问被告人。

公诉人经审判长许可，可以讯问被告人。

被害人、附带民事诉讼的原告人和辩护人，在审判人员审问被告人后，经审判长许可，可以向被告人发问。

第一百一十五条 审判人员、公诉人询问证人，应当告知他要如实地提供证言和有意作伪证或者隐匿罪证要负的法律责任。当事人和辩护人可以申请审判长对证人、鉴定人发问，或者请求审判长许可直接发问。审判长认为发问的内容与案件无关的时候，应当制止。

第一百一十六条 审判人员应当向被告人出示物证，让他辨认；对未到庭的证人的证言笔录、鉴定人的鉴定结论、勘验笔录和其他作为证据的文书，应当当庭宣读，并且听取当事人和辩护人的意见。

第一百一十七条 法庭审理过程中，当事人和辩护人有权申请通知新的证人到庭，调取新的物证，申请重新鉴定或者勘验。

法庭对于上述申请,应当作出是否同意的决定。

第一百一十八条 法庭调查后,应当由公诉人发言,被害人发言,然后由被告人陈述和辩护,辩护人进行辩护,并且可以互相辩论。审判长在宣布辩论终结后,被告人有最后陈述的权利。

第一百一十九条 在法庭审判过程中,如果诉讼参与人违反法庭秩序,审判长应当警告制止;情节严重的,可以责令退出法庭或者依法追究刑事责任。

第一百二十条 在被告人最后陈述后,审判长宣布休庭,合议庭进行评议,根据已经查明的事实、证据和有关的法律规定,作出被告人有罪或者无罪、犯的什么罪、适用什么刑罚或者免除刑罚的判决。

第一百二十一条 宣告判决,一律公开进行。

当庭宣告判决的,应当在五日以内将判决书送达当事人和提起公诉的人民检察院;定期宣告判决的,应当在宣告后立即将判决书送达当事人和提起公诉的人民检察院。

第一百二十二条 判决书应当由合议庭的组

成人员和书记员署名，并且写明上诉的期限和上诉的法院。

第一百二十三条 在法庭审判过程中，遇有下列情形之一影响审判进行的，可以延期审理：

（一）需要通知新的证人到庭，调取新的物证，重新鉴定或者勘验的；

（二）检察人员发现提起公诉的案件需要补充侦查，提出建议的；

（三）合议庭认为案件证据不充分，或者发现新的事实，需要退回人民检察院补充侦查或者自行调查的；

（四）由于当事人申请回避而不能进行审判的。

第一百二十四条 法庭审判的全部活动，应当由书记员写成笔录，经审判长审阅后，由审判长和书记员签名。

法庭笔录中的证人证言部分，应当当庭宣读或者交给证人阅读。证人在承认没有错误后，应当签名或者盖章。

法庭笔录应当交给当事人阅读或者向他宣读。当事人认为记载有遗漏或者差错的，可以请求补充或者改正。当事人承认没有错误后，应当签名或者盖章。

第一百二十五条 人民法院审理公诉案件,应当在受理后一个月内宣判,至迟不得超过一个半月。

第二节 自诉案件

第一百二十六条 人民法院对于自诉案件进行审查后,可以按照下列情形分别处理:

(一)犯罪事实清楚,有足够证据的案件,应当开庭审判;

(二)必须由人民检察院提起公诉的案件,应当移送人民检察院;

(三)缺乏罪证的自诉案件,如果自诉人提不出补充证据,经人民法院调查又未能收集到必要的证据,应当说服自诉人撤回自诉,或者裁定驳回;

(四)被告人的行为不构成犯罪的案件,应当说服自诉人撤回自诉,或者裁定驳回。

第一百二十七条 人民法院对自诉案件,可以进行调解;自诉人在宣告判决前,可以同被告人自行和解或者撤回自诉。

第一百二十八条 自诉案件的被告人在诉讼过程中,可以对自诉人提起反诉。反诉适用自诉的规定。

第三章　第二审程序

第一百二十九条　当事人或者他们的法定代理人，不服地方各级人民法院第一审的判决、裁定，有权用书状或者口头向上一级人民法院上诉。被告人的辩护人和近亲属，经被告人同意，可以提出上诉。

附带民事诉讼的当事人和他们的法定代理人，可以对地方各级人民法院第一审的判决、裁定中的附带民事诉讼部分，提出上诉。

对被告人的上诉权，不得以任何借口加以剥夺。

第一百三十条　地方各级人民检察院认为本级人民法院第一审的判决、裁定确有错误的时候，应当向上一级人民法院提出抗诉。

第一百三十一条　不服判决的上诉和抗诉的期限为十日，不服裁定的上诉和抗诉的期限为五日，从接到判决书、裁定书的第二日起算。

第一百三十二条　当事人通过原审人民法院提出上诉的，原审人民法院应当在三日以内将上诉状连同案卷、证据移送上一级人民法院，同时将上诉状副本送交同级人民检察院和对方当事人。

当事人直接向第二审人民法院提出上诉的，

第二审人民法院应当在三日以内将上诉状交原审人民法院送交同级人民检察院和对方当事人。

第一百三十三条 地方各级人民检察院对同级人民法院第一审判决、裁定的抗诉，应当通过原审人民法院提出抗诉书，并且将抗诉书抄送上一级人民检察院。原审人民法院应当将抗诉书连同案卷、证据移送上一级人民法院，并且将抗诉书副本送交当事人。

上级人民检察院如果认为抗诉不当，可以向同级人民法院撤回抗诉，并且通知下级人民检察院。

第一百三十四条 第二审人民法院应当就第一审判决认定的事实和适用法律进行全面审查，不受上诉或者抗诉范围的限制。

共同犯罪的案件只有部分被告人上诉的，应当对全案进行审查，一并处理。

第一百三十五条 人民检察院提出抗诉的案件或者第二审人民法院要求人民检察院派员出庭的案件，同级人民检察院都应当派员出庭。第二审人民法院必须在开庭十日以前通知人民检察院查阅案卷。

第一百三十六条 第二审人民法院对不服第一审判决的上诉、抗诉案件，经过审理后，应当按照下列情形分别处理：

（一）原判决认定事实和适用法律正确、量刑适当的，应当裁定驳回上诉或者抗诉，维持原判；

（二）原判决认定事实没有错误，但适用法律有错误，或者量刑不当的，应当改判；

（三）原判决事实不清楚或者证据不足的，可以在查清事实后改判；也可以裁定撤销原判，发回原审人民法院重新审判。

第一百三十七条 第二审人民法院审判被告人或者他的法定代理人、辩护人、近亲属上诉的案件，不得加重被告人的刑罚。

人民检察院提出抗诉或者自诉人提出上诉的，不受前款规定的限制。

第一百三十八条 第二审人民法院发现第一审人民法院违反法律规定的诉讼程序，可能影响正确判决的时候，应当撤销原判，发回原审人民法院重新审判。

第一百三十九条 原审人民法院对于发回重新审判的案件，应当依照第一审程序进行审判。对于重新审判后的判决，当事人可以上诉，同级人民检察院可以抗诉。

第一百四十条 第二审人民法院对不服第一审裁定的上诉或者抗诉，经过审查后，应当参照本法第一百三十六条、第一百三十八条和第一百三十九条的规定,分别情形用裁定驳回上诉、抗诉,或者撤销、变更原裁定。

第一百四十一条 第二审人民法院审判上诉或者抗诉案件的程序,除本章已有规定的以外,参照第一审程序的规定进行。

第一百四十二条 第二审人民法院受理上诉、抗诉案件后,应当在一个月以内审结,至迟不得超过一个半月。

第一百四十三条 第二审的判决、裁定和最高人民法院的判决、裁定,都是终审的判决、裁定。

第四章 死刑复核程序

第一百四十四条 死刑由最高人民法院核准。

第一百四十五条 中级人民法院判处死刑的第一审案件,被告人不上诉的,应由高级人民法院复核后,报请最高人民法院核准。高级人民法院不同意判处死刑的,可以提审或者发回重新审判。

高级人民法院判处死刑的第一审案件被告人不上诉的,和判处死刑的第二审案件,都应当报请最高人民法院核准。

第一百四十六条　中级人民法院判处死刑缓期二年执行的案件，由高级人民法院核准。

第一百四十七条　最高人民法院复核死刑案件，高级人民法院复核死刑缓期执行的案件，应当由审判员三人组成合议庭进行。

第五章　审判监督程序

第一百四十八条　当事人、被害人及其家属或者其他公民，对已经发生法律效力的判决、裁定，可以向人民法院或者人民检察院提出申诉，但不能停止判决、裁定的执行。

第一百四十九条　各级人民法院院长对本院已经发生法律效力的判决和裁定，如果发现在认定事实上或者在适用法律上确有错误，必须提交审判委员会处理。

最高人民法院对各级人民法院已经发生法律效力的判决和裁定，上级人民法院对下级人民法院已经发生法律效力的判决和裁定，如果发现确有错误，有权提审或者指令下级人民法院再审。

最高人民检察院对各级人民法院已经发生法律效力的判决和裁定，上级人民检察院对下级人民法院已经发生法律效力的判决和裁定，如果发现确有错误，有权按照审判监督程序提出抗诉。

第一百五十条 人民法院按照审判监督程序重新审判的案件,应当另行组成合议庭进行。如果原来是第一审案件,应当依照第一审程序进行审判,所作的判决、裁定,可以上诉、抗诉;如果原来是第二审案件,或者是上级人民法院提审的案件,应当依照第二审程序进行审判,所作的判决、裁定,是终审的判决、裁定。

第四编 执 行

第一百五十一条 判决和裁定在发生法律效力后执行。

下列判决和裁定是发生法律效力的判决和裁定：

（一）已过法定期限没有上诉、抗诉的判决和裁定；

（二）终审的判决和裁定；

（三）最高人民法院核准的死刑的判决和高级人民法院核准的死刑缓期二年执行的判决。

第一百五十二条 第一审人民法院判决被告人无罪、免除刑事处罚的，如果被告人在押，在宣判后应当立即释放。

第一百五十三条 最高人民法院判处和核准的死刑立即执行的判决，应当由最高人民法院院长签发执行死刑的命令。

被判处死刑缓期二年执行的罪犯，在死刑缓期执行期间，如果确有悔改或者有立功表现应当依法予以减刑的，由执行机关提出书面意见，报请当地高级人民法院裁定；如果抗拒改造情节恶劣、查证属实，应当执行死刑的，高级人民法院必须报请最高人民法院核准。

第一百五十四条 下级人民法院接到最高人民法院执行死刑的命令后，应当在七日以内交付执行。但是发现有下列情形之一的，应当停止执行，并且立即报告最高人民法院，由最高人民法院作出裁定：

（一）在执行前发现判决可能有错误的；

（二）罪犯正在怀孕。

前款第一项停止执行的原因消失后，必须报请最高人民法院院长再签发执行死刑的命令才能执行；由于前款第二项原因停止执行的，应当报请最高人民法院依法改判。

第一百五十五条 人民法院在交付执行死刑前，应当通知同级人民检察院派员临场监督。

指挥执行的审判人员，对罪犯应当验明正身，讯问有无遗言、信札，然后交付执行人员执行死刑。在执行前，如果发现可能有错误，应当暂停执行，报请最高人民法院裁定。

执行死刑应当公布，不应示众。

执行死刑后，在场书记员应当写成笔录。交付执行的人民法院应当将执行死刑情况报告最高人民法院。

执行死刑后,交付执行的人民法院应当通知罪犯家属。

第一百五十六条 对于被判处死刑缓期二年执行、无期徒刑、有期徒刑或者拘役的罪犯,应当由交付执行的人民法院将执行通知书、判决书送达监狱或者其他劳动改造场所执行,并且由执行机关通知罪犯家属。

判处有期徒刑、拘役的罪犯,执行期满,应当由执行机关发给刑满释放证。

第一百五十七条 对于被判处无期徒刑、有期徒刑或者拘役的罪犯,有下列情形之一的,可以暂予监外执行:

(一)有严重疾病需要保外就医的;

(二)怀孕或者正在哺乳自己婴儿的妇女。

对于监外执行的罪犯,可以由公安机关委托罪犯原居住地的公安派出所执行,基层组织或者原所在单位协助进行监督。

第一百五十八条 对于被判处徒刑缓刑的罪犯,由公安机关交所在单位或者基层组织予以考察。

对于被假释的罪犯,在假释考验期限内,由公安机关予以监督。

第一百五十九条 对于被判处管制、剥夺政治权利的罪犯,由公安机关执行。执行期满,应当由执行机关通知本人,并向有关群众公开宣布解除管制或者恢复政治权利。

第一百六十条 被判处罚金的罪犯,期满不缴纳的,人民法院应当强制缴纳;如果由于遭遇不能抗拒的灾祸缴纳确实有困难的,可以裁定减少或者免除。

第一百六十一条 没收财产的判决,无论附加适用或者独立适用,都由人民法院执行;在必要的时候,可以会同公安机关执行。

第一百六十二条 罪犯在服刑期间又犯罪的,或者发现了判决时所没有发现的罪行,监狱和劳动改造机关应当移送人民检察院处理。

被判处管制、拘役、有期徒刑或者无期徒刑的罪犯,在执行期间确有悔改或者立功表现,应当依法予以减刑、假释的时候,由执行机关提出书面意见,报请人民法院审核裁定。

第一百六十三条 监狱和劳动改造机关在刑罚执行中,如果认为判决有错误或者罪犯提出申诉,应当转请人民检察院或者原判人民法院处理。

第一百六十四条 人民检察院对刑事案件的判决、裁定的执行和监狱、看守所、劳动改造机关的活动是否合法,实行监督。如果发现有违法的情况,应当通知执行机关纠正。

APPENDICES
附 录

DECISION OF THE STANDING COMMITTEE OF THE NATIONAL PEOPLE'S CONGRESS REGARDING THE QUESTION OF APPROVAL OF CASES INVOLVING DEATH SENTENCES

(Adopted by the 19th Session of the Standing Committee of the Fifth National People's Congress, June 10, 1981)

In order promptly to attack such active criminal elements who seriously undermine public security as those who kill another, rob, commit rape, cause explosions or set fires, the following Decision is made with respect to the question of approval of cases involving death sentences:

1. Within the years 1981 to 1983, with respect to those who commit the crimes of killing another, robbery, rape, causing explosions, arson, spreading poisons, breaching dikes or undermining such equipment as transportation or electric power equipment, it is not necessary to submit to the Supreme People's Court for approval cases in which the high people's court of a province, autonomous region or municipality directly under the central government renders a judgment in the final instance of the death penalty, or those in which an intermediate people's

court renders a judgment in the first instance of the death penalty and the defendant does not appeal and the sentence is approved by a high people's court, or those in which a high people's court renders a judgment in the first instance of the death penalty and the defendant does not appeal.

2. With respect to sentences of death such as those imposed on offenders committing counterrevolution and offenders committing corruption, the Supreme People's Court is still to approve these in accordance with the stipulations of the Criminal Procedure Law regarding the procedure for review of death sentences.*

---

* On September 2, 1983, the Second Session of the Standing Committee of the Sixth National People's Congress adopted a relevant amendment to Article 13 of the Organic Law of the People's Courts of the People's Republic of China (1979). The original Article 13 of the Organic Law and the amended article follow respectively:

Article 13 In cases involving sentences of death, the sentences are to be rendered or approved by the Supreme People's Court. The procedure for review of cases involving sentences of death is to be handled in accordance with the stipulations of Chapter IV of Part III of the Criminal Procedure Law of the People's Republic of China.

Article 13 (as amended) In cases involving sentences of death, the sentences, except those rendered by the Supreme People's Court, shall be reported to the Supreme People's Court for approval. In cases of killing another, rape, robbery, causing explosions and other cases of serious endangerment to public safety and public security in which death sentences are imposed, the Supreme People's Court, when necessary, is to authorize the high people's courts of the provinces, autonomous regions and municipalities directly under the central government with the exercise of the right of approval. — *Trans.*

全国人民代表大会常务委员会
关于死刑案件核准问题的决定

（一九八一年六月十日第五届全国人民代表大会常务委员会第十九次会议通过）

为了及时打击现行的杀人、抢劫、强奸、爆炸、放火等严重破坏社会治安的犯罪分子，现对死刑案件核准问题，作如下决定：

一、在一九八一年至一九八三年内，对犯有杀人、抢劫、强奸、爆炸、放火、投毒、决水和破坏交通、电力等设备的罪行，由省、自治区、直辖市高级人民法院终审判决死刑的，或者中级人民法院一审判决死刑，被告人不上诉，经高级人民法院核准的，以及高级人民法院一审判决死刑，被告人不上诉的，都不必报最高人民法院核准。

二、对反革命犯和贪污犯等判处死刑，仍然按照刑事诉讼法关于死刑复核程序的规定，由最高人民法院核准。

DECISION OF THE STANDING COMMITTEE OF THE NATIONAL PEOPLE'S CONGRESS REGARDING THE HANDLING OF OFFENDERS UNDERGOING REFORM THROUGH LABOUR AND PERSONS UNDERGOING REHABILITATION THROUGH LABOUR WHO ESCAPE OR COMMIT NEW CRIMES

(Adopted by the 19th Session of the Standing Committee of the Fifth National People's Congress, June 10, 1981)

Among the criminal elements who are currently seriously endangering public security, there is a considerable group who have escaped from places of reform through labour or rehabilitation through labour* or who have continued to commit crimes after

---

* "Reform through labour" (*laodong gaizao*) is a form of criminal punishment, referred to in the Criminal Law and Criminal Procedure Law, used generally for those who are sentenced to fixed-term imprisonment or life imprisonment and who can work. "Rehabilitation through labour" (*laodong jiaoyang*) is a non-criminal, administrative sanction. Its legal basis lies not in the Criminal Law or Criminal Procedure Law but in the Decision of the State Council Regarding the Question of Rehabilitation Through Labour, approved by the 78th Session of the Standing Committee of the First

release upon the completion of their term, and who do not reform after repeated education. In order to maintain public security and strengthen the education and reform of offenders undergoing reform through labour and persons undergoing rehabilitation through labour, the following Decision is specially made:

1. Extension of the period of rehabilitation through labour for persons undergoing rehabilitation through labour who escape.

Persons undergoing rehabilitation through labour who commit crimes within three years after their release from rehabilitation, and those who commit crimes within five years after escaping are to be given a heavier punishment, and to have their city residence registration cancelled. Upon the completion of their term, except for those who have actually reformed, such offenders are in all cases to remain

---

National People's Congress, August 1, 1957, promulgated by the State Council, August 3, 1957; and the Supplementary Provisions of the State Council Regarding Rehabilitation Through Labour, approved by the 12th Session of the Standing Committee of the Fifth National People's Congress, November 29, 1979, promulgated by the State Council, November 29, 1979. Under these documents, able-bodied individuals who engage in unlawful conduct such as theft for which it is decided not to use criminal sanctions may be sent for up to three years of rehabilitation through labour in a special place of rehabilitation by an administrative committee of rehabilitation through labour composed of representatives of the civil affairs, public security and labour departments. The term of rehabilitation through labour may be extended to up to four years. Persons undergoing rehabilitation through labour are to receive appropriate compensation for their work. The procuratorates are to exercise supervision over organs of rehabilitation through labour. — *Trans.*

at the place of rehabilitation and be employed and may not return to their large or medium-sized cities of origin. Those among them the circumstances of whose cases are minor, not qualifying for criminal sanctions, are to undergo rehabilitation through labour again or have their period of rehabilitation extended and may have their city residence registration cancelled. Upon completion of their term, they are in general to remain at the place of rehabilitation and be employed and may not return to their large or medium-sized cities of origin.

2. For offenders undergoing reform through labour who escape, besides executing their sentences in accordance with the term originally imposed, fixed-term imprisonment of not more than five years is to be imposed in addition; for those who escape by violent or threatening methods, fixed-term imprisonment of not less than two years and not more than seven years is to be imposed in addition.

Offenders undergoing reform through labour who again commit crimes after escaping are to be given a heavier punishment or a punishment beyond the maximum prescribed; those who again commit crimes after release upon the completion of their term are to be given a heavier punishment. In all cases, the above offenders are to remain at the place of reform and be employed after the completion of their term and may not return to their large or medium-sized cities of origin.

Where, after release upon completion of a term of reform through labour, there are minor criminal acts, not qualifying for criminal sanctions, the offender is to be given the sanction of rehabilitation through labour. Offenders are in general to remain at the place of reform and be employed after the completion of their term and may not return to their large or medium-sized cities of origin.

Criminals undergoing reform through labour who have not reformed are to remain at the place of reform and be employed after the completion of their term of reform through labour.

3. Persons undergoing rehabilitation through labour or criminals undergoing reform through labour who in retaliation do violence against their accusers, victims, relevant judicial personnel and cadres and people who put a stop to their illegal criminal acts are to be given a heavier punishment or a punishment beyond the maximum prescribed in accordance with the stipulations of law on the crimes they have committed.

4. This decision is to be implemented from July 10, 1981.

全国人民代表大会常务委员会关于处理逃跑或者重新犯罪的劳改犯和劳教人员的决定

(一九八一年六月十日第五届全国人民代表大会常务委员会第十九次会议通过)

目前严重危害社会治安的犯罪分子中,有相当一批是从劳动改造、劳动教养场所逃跑或者期满释放后继续犯罪,屡教不改的。为了维护社会治安,加强对劳改犯和劳教人员的教育改造,特作如下决定:

一、劳教人员逃跑的,延长劳教期限。

劳教人员解除教养后三年内犯罪、逃跑后五年内犯罪的,从重处罚,并且注销本人城市户口,期满后除确实改造好的以外,一律留场就业,不得回原大中城市。其中情节轻微、不够刑事处分的,重新劳动教养或者延长劳动教养期限,并且可以注销本人城市户口,期满后一般留场就业,不得回原大中城市。

二、劳改犯逃跑的,除按原判刑期执行外,

加处五年以下有期徒刑；以暴力、威胁方法逃跑的，加处二年以上七年以下有期徒刑。

劳改犯逃跑后又犯罪的，从重或者加重处罚；刑满释放后又犯罪的，从重处罚。刑满后一律留场就业，不得回原大中城市。

劳改期满释放后，有轻微犯罪行为、不够刑事处分的，给予劳动教养处分。期满后一般留场就业，不得回原大中城市。

没有改造好的劳改罪犯，劳改期满后留场就业。

三、劳教人员、劳改罪犯对检举人、被害人和有关的司法工作人员以及制止违法犯罪行为的干部、群众行凶报复的，按照其所犯罪行的法律规定，从重或者加重处罚。

四、本决定自一九八一年七月十日起施行。

DECISION OF THE STANDING COMMITTEE OF THE NATIONAL PEOPLE'S CONGRESS REGARDING THE QUESTION OF THE TIME LIMITS FOR HANDLING CRIMINAL CASES

(Adopted by the 20th Session of the Standing Committee of the Fifth National People's Congress, September 10, 1981)

Since 1981, various localities throughout the country have begun comprehensively to carry out the time limits for handling cases stipulated in the Criminal Procedure Law. The great majority of criminal cases can be completed within the legally prescribed time limits. However, there is still a small number of criminal cases the circumstances of which are complex or which involve remote areas for which transportation is inconvenient, which, being hampered by such conditions as manpower and transportation, cannot be completed within the legally prescribed time limits. For this reason, according to the suggestion of the Supreme People's Procuratorate and the Supreme People's Court, the 20th Session of the Standing Committee of the Fifth National People's Congress has decided that criminal cases accepted on or after January 1, 1981 shall in general be handled in accordance with the time limits for handling cases stipulated in the Criminal Procedure Law, and that with respect to a small number of criminal cases the circumstances of which are complex or which involve remote areas for which transportation is inconvenient, which cannot be handled in accordance with the time limits regarding investigation, prosecution, adjudication of first instance, and adjudication of second instance stipulated in the Criminal Procedure Law, within the years 1981 to 1983, the standing committees of the people's congresses of the provinces, autonomous regions and municipalities directly under the central government may decide upon or approve appropriate extended time limits for handling cases.

全国人民代表大会常务委员会
关于刑事案件办案期限问题的决定

（一九八一年九月十日第五届全国人民代表大会常务委员会第二十次会议通过）

一九八一年以来，全国各地开始全面执行刑事诉讼法规定的办案期限，大多数刑事案件都能在法定期限内办结。但是仍有少数案情复杂或者交通不便的边远地区的刑事案件，因受人力、交通等条件的限制，在法定期限内不能办结。为此，根据最高人民检察院和最高人民法院的建议，第五届全国人民代表大会常务委员会第二十次会议决定：一九八一年一月一日以后受理的刑事案件，一般应当依照刑事诉讼法规定的办案期限办理；少数案情复杂或者交通不便的边远地区的刑事案件，不能按照刑事诉讼法规定的关于侦查、起诉、一审、二审的期限办理的，在一九八一年至一九八三年内，可以由省、自治区、直辖市的人民代表大会常务委员会决定或者批准适当延长办案期限。

DECISION OF THE STANDING COMMITTEE OF THE NATIONAL PEOPLE'S CONGRESS REGARDING THE SEVERE PUNISHMENT OF CRIMINALS WHO SERIOUSLY UNDERMINE THE ECONOMY

(Adopted by the 22nd Session of the Standing Committee of the Fifth National People's Congress, March 8, 1982)

In view of the fact that currently economic criminal activities such as seeking exorbitant profits through smuggling, speculative arbitrage and speculation, theft of articles of public property, theft and sale of precious cultural relics and extortion and acceptance of bribes are rampant, with serious harm to the cause of the country's socialist construction and to the interests of the people, and in order resolutely to attack such criminal activities and severely to punish these criminal elements and state personnel who participate in, protect or connive at these criminal activities, there is the necessity of making appropriate supplementations and revisions to some relevant provisions of the Criminal Law of the People's Republic of China. It is hereby decided as follows:

I. The following supplementations and revisions

are to be made to the relevant provisions of the Criminal Law:

(1) With respect to the crimes of seeking exorbitant profits through smuggling, speculative arbitrage and speculation in Article 118 of the Criminal Law, the crime of theft in Article 152, the crime of sale of narcotics in Article 171, the crime of stealing and exporting precious cultural relics in Article 173, their sentencing is respectively supplemented or revised as follows: when the circumstances are particularly serious, the sentence is to be not less than ten years of fixed-term imprisonment, life imprisonment or death, and the offender may in addition be sentenced to confiscation of property.

State personnel who take advantage of their office to commit the crimes listed in the preceding paragraph, when the circumstances are particularly serious, are to be given a heavier punishment in accordance with the stipulations of the preceding paragraph. State personnel referred to in this decision include personnel working in state organs of power at all levels, administrative organs at all levels, judicial organs at all levels, the armed forces, state enterprises, and state institutional organizations, and other personnel of all types who are engaged in public service according to law.

(2) With respect to the crime of acceptance of bribes in Article 185, Paragraphs 1 and 2, of the Criminal Law, the stipulations are revised as follows: cases involving state personnel who extort or accept bribes are to be handled according to the crime of corruption in Article 155 of the Criminal Law; when

the circumstances are particularly serious, the sentence is to be life imprisonment or death.

(3) State personnel, irrespective of whether or not they are judicial personnel, who take advantage of their office to protect or harbour criminal elements as stipulated in (1) and (2) of this Article, concealing and covering up the facts of their crimes, are all to be punished in accordance with the stipulations of Article 188 of the Criminal Law on the crime of self-seeking misconduct.

Relatives of state personnel or state personnel who have already left office who commit the above crimes are to be punished in accordance with the stipulations of Article 162, Paragraph 2, of the Criminal Law on the crime of protection.

Whoever destroys criminal evidence or fabricates false evidence for the above criminal elements is to be punished in accordance with the stipulations of Article 148 of the Criminal Law on the crime of false evidence.

Whoever carries on thwarting, threats or retaliatory attacks on law enforcement personnel and personnel who expose, accuse and give testimony is to be punished in accordance with the stipulations of Article 157 of the Criminal Law on the crime of disrupting the order of social administration or those of Article 146 on the crime of retaliation or frame-ups.

If, before committing the crimes in the preceding four paragraphs, the offender conspires with the criminals listed in (1) and (2) of this Article, the matter is to be handled as a joint crime.

(4) With respect to criminals listed in (1), (2) and (3) of this Article, if state personnel with the responsibility for investigation do not handle the matter according to law, or if, because they are thwarted, do not perform the investigatory obligations stipulated by law; and with respect to personnel directly in charge who know the circumstances of criminals and of the facts of crimes or the personnel with the only knowledge of these circumstances who do not report the case according to law and do not give testimony truthfully, punishment is to be given respectively according to the crimes of dereliction of duty stipulated in Articles 187, 188 and 190 of the Criminal Law.

II. This Decision is to be implemented from April 1, 1982.

Any cases of crimes committed on or before the date of implementation of this Decision in which on or before May 1, 1982 the offender voluntarily surrenders, or, if he has already been arrested, truthfully confesses and acknowledges the entirety of his crimes, and in addition truthfully brings accusations with respect to the facts of crimes of other criminals, are all to be handled in accordance with the relevant stipulations of law before the implementation of this Decision. Any cases in which the offender, on or before May 1, 1982, continues to conceal the crimes he has committed, refusing to surrender voluntarily, or refuses to confess and acknowledge the entirety of his crimes, and also does not bring accusations with respect to the facts of crimes of other criminals, are to be taken as the continuing commission of crimes and are all to be handled in accordance with this Decision.

III. This Decision has a major bearing on the interests of the state and the entire people. From the date of promulgation of this Decision, all state organs, the armed forces, enterprises, institutional organizations, rural people's communes and production brigades, party organizations, people's organizations, schools, newspapers, broadcasting stations and other propaganda units have the duty to adopt every effective method repeatedly to carry on commonly understandable propaganda and explanations for the entire corps of working personnel, army officers and men, staff and workers, students and urban and rural residents, to make this Decision a household word known to everyone.*

---

* Appended to this Decision is a list of all the articles of the Criminal Law affected by the Decision. These are not translated again here, but may be identified by the symbol "†" in the translation of the Criminal Law, *supra.* — *Trans.*

全国人民代表大会常务委员会关于严惩严重破坏经济的罪犯的决定

(一九八二年三月八日第五届全国人民代表大会常务委员会第二十二次会议通过)

鉴于当前走私、套汇、投机倒把牟取暴利、盗窃公共财物、盗卖珍贵文物和索贿受贿等经济犯罪活动猖獗，对国家社会主义建设事业和人民利益危害严重，为了坚决打击这些犯罪活动，严厉惩处这些犯罪分子和参与、包庇或者纵容这些犯罪活动的国家工作人员，有必要对《中华人民共和国刑法》的一些有关条款作相应的补充和修改。现决定如下：

一、对刑法有关条款作下列补充和修改：

（一）对刑法第一百一十八条走私、套汇、投机倒把牟取暴利罪，第一百五十二条盗窃罪，第一百七十一条贩毒罪，第一百七十三条盗运珍贵文物出口罪，其处刑分别补充或者修改为：情节严重的，处十年以上有期徒刑、无期徒刑或者死刑，可以并处没收财产。

国家工作人员利用职务犯前款所列罪行，情节特别严重的，按前款规定从重处罚。本决定所称国家工作人员，包括在国家各级权力机关、各级行政机关、各级司法机关、军队、国营企业、国家事业机构中工作的人员，以及其他各种依照法律从事公务的人员。

（二）对刑法第一百八十五条第一款和第二款受贿罪修改规定为：国家工作人员索取、收受贿赂的，比照刑法第一百五十五条贪污罪论处；情节特别严重的，处无期徒刑或者死刑。

（三）国家工作人员，无论是否司法人员，利用职务包庇、窝藏本条（一）、（二）规定的犯罪分子，隐瞒、掩饰他们的犯罪事实的，都按刑法第一百八十八条徇私舞弊罪的规定处罚；

国家工作人员的亲属或者已离职的国家工作人员，犯上述罪行的，按刑法第一百六十二条第二款包庇罪的规定处罚；

为上述犯罪分子销毁罪证或者制造伪证的，按刑法第一百四十八条伪证罪的规定处罚；

对执法人员和揭发、检举、作证人员进行阻挠、威胁、打击报复的，按刑法第一百五十七条妨害社会管理秩序罪或者第一百四十六条报复陷害罪的规定处罚。

犯前四款罪，事前与本条（一）、（二）所列举的罪犯通谋的，以共同犯罪论处。

（四）对于本条（一）、（二）、（三）所列的犯罪人员，有追究责任的国家工作人员不依法处理，或者因受阻挠而不履行法律所规定的追究职责的；对犯罪人员和犯罪事实知情的直接主管人员或者仅有的知情的工作人员不依法报案和不如实作证的，分别比照刑法第一百八十七条、第一百八十八条、第一百九十条所规定的渎职罪处罚。

二、本决定自一九八二年四月一日起施行。

凡在本决定施行之日以前犯罪，而在一九八二年五月一日以前投案自首，或者已被逮捕而如实地坦白承认全部罪行，并如实地检举其他犯罪人员的犯罪事实的，一律按本决定施行以前的有关法律规定处理。凡在一九八二年五月一日以前对所犯的罪行继续隐瞒拒不投案自首，或者拒不坦白承认本人的全部罪行，亦不检举其他犯罪人员的犯罪事实的，作为继续犯罪，一律按本决定处理。

三、本决定对国家和全体人民利益关系重大，所有国家机关、军队、企业、事业机构、农村社队、政党组织、人民团体、学校、报纸、电台和其他宣传单位，自本决定公布之日起，都有义务采取一切有效方法，对全体工作人员、指战员、职工、学生和城乡居民，反复进行通俗的宣传解释，做到家喻户晓，人人皆知。

附：刑法有关条文

第一百一十八条 以走私、投机倒把为常业的，走私、投机倒把数额巨大的或者走私、投机倒把集团的首要分子，处三年以上十年以下有期徒刑，可以并处没收财产。

第一百五十二条 惯窃、惯骗或者盗窃、诈骗、抢夺公私财物数额巨大的，处五年以上十年以下有期徒刑；情节特别严重的，处十年以上有期徒刑或者无期徒刑，可以并处没收财产。

第一百七十一条 制造、贩卖、运输鸦片、海洛英、吗啡或者其他毒品的，处五年以下有期徒刑或者拘役，可以并处罚金。

一贯或者大量制造、贩卖、运输前款毒品的，处五年以上有期徒刑，可以并处没收财产。

第一百七十三条 违反保护文物法规，盗运珍贵文物出口的，处三年以上十年以下有期徒刑，可以并处罚金；情节严重的，处十年以上有期徒刑或者无期徒刑，可以并处没收财产。

第一百八十五条 国家工作人员利用职务上的便利,收受贿赂的,处五年以下有期徒刑或者拘役。赃款、赃物没收,公款、公物追还。

犯前款罪,致使国家或者公民利益遭受严重损失的,处五年以上有期徒刑。

向国家工作人员行贿或者介绍贿赂的,处三年以下有期徒刑或者拘役。

第一百五十五条 国家工作人员利用职务上的便利,贪污公共财物的,处五年以下有期徒刑或者拘役;数额巨大、情节严重的,处五年以上有期徒刑;情节特别严重的,处无期徒刑或者死刑。

犯前款罪的,并处没收财产,或者判令退赔。

受国家机关、企业、事业单位、人民团体委托从事公务的人员犯第一款罪的,依照前两款的规定处罚。

第一百八十八条 司法工作人员徇私舞弊,对明知是无罪的人而使他受追诉、对明知是有罪的人而故意包庇不使他受追诉,或者故意颠倒黑白做枉法裁判的,处五年以下有期徒刑、拘役或者剥夺政治权利;情节特别严重的,处五年以上有期徒刑。

第一百六十二条 窝藏或者作假证明包庇反革命分子的，处三年以下有期徒刑、拘役或者管制；情节严重的，处三年以上十年以下有期徒刑。

窝藏或者作假证明包庇其他犯罪分子的，处二年以下有期徒刑、拘役或者管制；情节严重的，处二年以上七年以下有期徒刑。

犯前两款罪，事前通谋的，以共同犯罪论处。

第一百四十八条 在侦查、审判中，证人、鉴定人、记录人、翻译人对与案件有重要关系的情节，故意作虚假证明、鉴定、记录、翻译，意图陷害他人或者隐匿罪证的，处二年以下有期徒刑或者拘役；情节严重的，处二年以上七年以下有期徒刑。

第一百五十七条 以暴力、威胁方法阻碍国家工作人员依法执行职务的，或者拒不执行人民法院已经发生法律效力的判决、裁定的，处三年以下有期徒刑、拘役、罚金或者剥夺政治权利。

第一百四十六条 国家工作人员滥用职权、假公济私，对控告人、申诉人、批评人实行报复陷害的，处二年以下有期徒刑或者拘役；情节严重的，处二年以上七年以下有期徒刑。

第一百八十七条 国家工作人员由于玩忽职

守，致使公共财产、国家和人民利益遭受重大损失的，处五年以下有期徒刑或者拘役。

第一百九十条 司法工作人员私放罪犯的，处五年以下有期徒刑或者拘役；情节严重的，处五年以上十年以下有期徒刑。

DECISION OF THE STANDING COMMITTEE OF THE NATIONAL PEOPLE'S CONGRESS REGARDING THE SEVERE PUNISHMENT OF CRIMINAL ELEMENTS WHO SERIOUSLY ENDANGER PUBLIC SECURITY

(Adopted by the Second Session of the Standing Committee of the Sixth National People's Congress, September 2, 1983)

In order to maintain public security, protect the safety of the lives and property of the people and safeguard the smooth progress of socialist construction, it is necessary to apply severe punishment to criminal elements that seriously endanger public security. To this end it is decided:

1. With respect to the following criminal elements who seriously endanger public security, punishment above the maximum punishment stipulated in the Criminal Law may be imposed, up to and including imposition of death sentences:

(1) Ringleaders of criminal hooligan groups or those who carry lethal weapons to engage in criminal hooligan activities, when the circumstances are serious, or those who engage in criminal hooligan activities resulting in especially serious harm;

(2) Those who intentionally injure the persons of others, causing a person's serious injury or death, when the circumstances are odious, or those who

commit violence and do injury to state personnel and citizens who accuse, expose or arrest criminal elements and stop criminal conduct;

(3) ' Ringleaders of groups that abduct and sell people, or those who abduct and sell people when the circumstances are especially serious;

(4) Those who illegally manufacture, trade in, transport, steal or forcibly seize guns, ammunition or explosives, when the circumstances are especially serious or when serious consequences are caused;

(5) Those who organize reactionary superstitious sects and secret societies, and use feudal superstition to carry on counterrevolutionary activities, seriously endangering public security;

(6) Those who lure women into prostitution, shelter them in prostitution, or force them into prostitution, when the circumstances are especially serious.

2. Whoever imparts criminal methods, when the circumstances are relatively minor, is to be sentenced to not more than five years of fixed-term imprisonment; when the circumstances are serious, the sentence is to be not less than five years of fixed-term imprisonment; when the circumstances are especially serious, the sentence is to be life imprisonment or death.

3. In adjudicating the above criminal cases after the promulgation of this Decision, this Decision is to be applied.*

---

* Appended to this Decision is a list of all the articles of the Criminal Law affected by the Decision. These are not translated again here, but may be identified by the symbol "††" in the translation of the Criminal Law, *supra*. — *Trans.*

全国人民代表大会常务委员会关于严惩严重危害社会治安的犯罪分子的决定

(一九八三年九月二日第六届全国人民代表大会常务委员会第二次会议通过)

为了维护社会治安,保护人民生命、财产的安全,保障社会主义建设的顺利进行,对严重危害社会治安的犯罪分子必须予以严惩。为此决定:

一、对下列严重危害社会治安的犯罪分子,可以在刑法规定的最高刑以上处刑,直至判处死刑:

1. 流氓犯罪集团的首要分子或者携带凶器进行流氓犯罪活动,情节严重的,或者进行流氓犯罪活动危害特别严重的;

2. 故意伤害他人身体,致人重伤或者死亡,情节恶劣的,或者对检举、揭发、拘捕犯罪分子和制止犯罪行为的国家工作人员和公民行凶伤害的;

3.拐卖人口集团的首要分子，或者拐卖人口情节特别严重的；

4.非法制造、买卖、运输或者盗窃、抢夺枪支、弹药、爆炸物，情节特别严重的，或者造成严重后果的；

5.组织反动会道门，利用封建迷信，进行反革命活动，严重危害社会治安的；

6.引诱、容留、强迫妇女卖淫，情节特别严重的。

二、传授犯罪方法，情节较轻的，处五年以下有期徒刑；情节严重的，处五年以上有期徒刑；情节特别严重的，处无期徒刑或者死刑。

三、本决定公布后审判上述犯罪案件，适用本决定。

附件：

刑法有关条文

第一百六十条 聚众斗殴，寻衅滋事，侮辱妇女或者进行其他流氓活动，破坏公共秩序，情节恶劣的，处七年以下有期徒刑、拘役或者管制。

流氓集团的首要分子，处七年以上有期徒刑。

第一百三十四条 故意伤害他人身体的，处三年以下有期徒刑或者拘役。

犯前款罪,致人重伤的,处三年以上七年以下有期徒刑;致人死亡的,处七年以上有期徒刑或者无期徒刑。本法另有规定的,依照规定。

第一百四十一条 拐卖人口的,处五年以下有期徒刑;情节严重的,处五年以上有期徒刑。

第一百一十二条 非法制造、买卖、运输枪支、弹药的,或者盗窃、抢夺国家机关、军警人员、民兵的枪支、弹药的,处七年以下有期徒刑;情节严重的,处七年以上有期徒刑或者无期徒刑。

第九十九条 组织、利用封建迷信、会道门进行反革命活动的,处五年以上有期徒刑;情节较轻的,处五年以下有期徒刑、拘役、管制或者剥夺政治权利。

第一百四十条 强迫妇女卖淫的,处三年以上十年以下有期徒刑。

第一百六十九条 以营利为目的,引诱、容留妇女卖淫的,处五年以下有期徒刑、拘役或者管制;情节严重的,处五年以上有期徒刑,可以并处罚金或者没收财产。

DECISION OF THE STANDING COMMITTEE OF THE NATIONAL PEOPLE'S CONGRESS REGARDING THE PROCEDURE FOR RAPID ADJUDICATION OF CASES INVOLVING CRIMINAL ELEMENTS WHO SERIOUSLY ENDANGER PUBLIC SECURITY

(Adopted by the Second Session of the Standing Committee of the Sixth National People's Congress, September 2, 1983)

In order rapidly and severely to punish criminal elements who seriously endanger public security, to protect the interests of the state and the people, it is decided:

1. With respect to criminal elements on whom death sentences should be imposed for killing another, rape, robbery, causing explosions, and other serious endangerment to public security, where the main criminal facts are clear and the evidence irrefutable and the people's indignation is very great, the case should be rapidly and promptly adjudicated, and [the people's courts] may not be bound by the restrictions stipulated by Article 110 of the Criminal Procedure Law regarding the time limit for delivery to the defendant of a copy of the

bill of prosecution and the time limits for the delivery of various subpoenas and notices.

2. The time limit for appeal by the criminal elements listed in the preceding paragraph and the time limit for protest by the people's procuratorates is changed to 3 days from the 10 days stipulated in Article 131 of the Criminal Procedure Law.*

---

* Appended to this Decision are the articles of the Criminal Procedure Law affected by the Decision, i.e., Articles 110 (Clauses 2, 3, 4) and 131. These are not translated again here. -- *Trans*.

全国人民代表大会常务委员会关于迅速审判严重危害社会治安的犯罪分子的程序的决定

（一九八三年九月二日第六届全国人民代表大会常务委员会第二次会议通过）

为了迅速严惩严重危害社会治安的犯罪分子，保护国家和人民的利益，决定：

一、对杀人、强奸、抢劫、爆炸和其他严重危害公共安全应当判处死刑的犯罪分子，主要犯罪事实清楚，证据确凿，民愤极大的，应当迅速及时审判，可以不受刑事诉讼法第一百一十条规定的关于起诉书副本送达被告人期限以及各项传票、通知书送达期限的限制。

二、前条所列犯罪分子的上诉期限和人民检察院的抗诉期限，由刑事诉讼法第一百三十一条规定的十日改为三日。

附件：
刑事诉讼法有关条文

第一百一十条 人民法院决定开庭审判后，应当进行下列工作：

……

（二）将人民检察院的起诉书副本至迟在开庭七日以前送达被告人，并且告知被告人可以委托辩护人，或者在必要时为被告人指定辩护人；

（三）将开庭的时间、地点在开庭三日以前通知人民检察院；

（四）传唤当事人，通知辩护人、证人、鉴定人和翻译人员，传票和通知书至迟在开庭三日以前送达；

……

第一百三十一条 不服判决的上诉和抗诉的期限为十日，不服裁定的上诉和抗诉的期限为五日，从接到判决书、裁定书的第二日起算。

DECISION OF THE STANDING COMMITTEE OF THE NATIONAL PEOPLE'S CONGRESS REGARDING THE EXERCISE BY THE STATE SECURITY ORGANS OF THE PUBLIC SECURITY ORGANS' POWERS OF INVESTIGATION, DETENTION, PREPARATORY EXAMINATION AND CARRYING OUT ARREST

(Adopted by the Second Session of the Standing Committee of the Sixth National People's Congress, September 2, 1983)

The state security organs established by decision of the First Session of the Sixth National People's Congress are to undertake the investigatory work concerning cases of espionage and special agents of which the public security organs were originally in charge, and are of the nature of state public security organs. Therefore, the state security organs may exercise the public security organs' powers of investigation, detention, preparatory examination and carrying out arrest as stipulated by the Constitution and by law.

全国人民代表大会常务委员会关于国家安全机关行使公安机关的侦查、拘留、预审和执行逮捕的职权的决定

（一九八三年九月二日第六届全国人民代表大会常务委员会第二次会议通过）

第六届全国人民代表大会第一次会议决定设立的国家安全机关，承担原由公安机关主管的间谍、特务案件的侦查工作，是国家公安机关的性质，因而国家安全机关可以行使宪法和法律规定的公安机关的侦查、拘留、预审和执行逮捕的职权。

ENGLISH-CHINESE GLOSSARY
英汉词汇对照表

A

abduct 拐骗
abduct and sell people 拐卖人口
abuse 虐待
abuse one's powers 滥用职权
accept (a case) 受理（案件）
accept a bribe 受贿
accomplice 从犯
accusation at variance with the facts 检举失实
accuse 检举
accuser 检举人
act of sabotage 破坏行为
act that subjects one's person to indignity 人身侮辱的行为
active criminal 现行犯
(in) addition be sentenced to ... 并处
addressee 收件人
adjudicate; adjudication 审判
adjudication committee 审判委员会
administrative sanction 行政处分
affirm the original judgment 维持原判
aid an enemy 资敌
alter official documents 变造公文

ammunition 军火
analagous 类似
announcement of not guilty 宣告无罪
appeal 上诉
appeal petition 上诉状
appealed case 上诉案件
appear in court 出庭
application for approval of arrest 提请批准逮捕书
apply (a punishment) in a supplementary manner 附加适用
apply (a punishment) in an independent manner 独立适用
apprehend 查获
armed mass rebellion 持械聚众叛乱
arms 武器
arrange a settlement 和解
arrest 逮捕
arrest warrant 逮捕证
arson 放火
article of property 财物
article of public property 公共财物
assemble a crowd to commit a crime 聚众犯罪
autopsy 解剖

B

basic people's court 基层人民法院
beat 殴打
beat, smash and loot 打、砸、抢
become effective 生效
big character poster 大字报
bigamy 重婚

bill of prosecution　起诉书
bogus medicine　假药
booty　赃物
boundary marker　界桩
boundary tablet　界碑
brawl　斗殴
breach dikes　决水
bribe　贿赂；收买
bring up and adjudicate (a case)　提审

C

cancel one's residence registration　注销户口
carry out　执行
case　案件
case of private prosecution　自诉案件
case of public prosecution　公诉案件
cause a person's injury or disability　致人伤残
cause explosions　爆炸
cause serious injury (death) to a person　致人重伤（死亡）
certificate of completion of sentence and release　刑满释放证
charge　罪名
cheat and bluff　招摇撞骗
chief judge　审判长
chief procurator　检察长
circumstances of a case are major or complex　案情重大、复杂
circumstances of a crime　犯罪情节
citizens' lawful privately-owned property　公民私人所有的合法财产

clerk 书记员
coerce 胁迫
coercive measure 强制措施
cohabit 同居
collegial panel 合议庭
collude with foreign states 勾结外国
collude with others to devise a consistent story 串供
combine punishment with leniency 惩办与宽大相结合
combined punishment for more than one crime 数罪并罚
commit a new crime 重新犯罪
complain 控告；告诉
complainant 控告人
conceal booty 窝藏赃物
conceal criminal evidence 隐匿罪证
confess and acknowledge (one's crimes) 坦白承认（罪行）
confiscation of property 没收财产
connive at 纵容
conspire 通谋
(one who) consummates a crime 既遂犯
contraband 违禁品
control 管制
coordinate with each other and restrain each other 互相配合，互相制约
corporal punishment 肉刑；体罚
(crime of) corruption 贪污（罪）
corruption involving articles of public property 贪污公共财物
counterclaim 反诉

counterfeit national currency 伪造国家货币
counterfeit valuable securities 伪造有价证券
(crime of) counterrevolution 反革命（罪）
counterrevolutionary element 反革命分子
credence should not be readily given to oral statements 不轻信口供
(commit a) crime 犯罪
criminal 罪犯；犯人；犯罪人
criminal act （刑事）犯罪行为
criminal activity 犯罪活动
criminal attempt 犯罪未遂
criminal detention 拘役
criminal element 犯罪分子
criminal evidence 罪证
criminal group 犯罪集团
criminal law 刑法
criminal procedure 刑事诉讼
criminal procedure law 刑事诉讼法
criminal punishment 刑罚；刑罚处罚
criminal responsibility 刑事责任
criminal sanction 刑事处分
criminal suspect 犯罪嫌疑人
criminal undergoing reform through labour 劳改犯
cross-examination 质证
cruelly injure or slaughter draft animals 残害耕畜
custody 关押

D

damage 损毁；损害
danger prevention 防险
deaf-mute 又聋又哑的人

death penalty 死刑
death penalty with a suspension of execution 死刑缓期执行
death sentence 死刑
deception 欺骗
decide (by judgment) 判决
decision to exempt from prosecution 免予起诉决定书
decree 法令
defame; defamation 诽谤
defect to the enemy and turn traitor 投敌叛变
defence 辩护
defence lawyer 辩护律师
defendant 被告人
defender 辩护人
deliberation 评议
democratic rights 民主权利
demonstrate meritorious service 有立功表现
demonstrate repentance 有悔罪表现
denude forests 滥伐森林
deportation 驱逐出境
deprivation of political rights 剥夺政治权利
(crime of) dereliction of duty 渎职（罪）
destroy criminal evidence 毁灭罪证
detain 拘留；拘禁
detention house 看守所
detention warrant 拘留证
determine a case 定案
determine a crime 定罪
diplomatic privilege 外交特权
disclose state secrets 泄露国家机密
discontinuation of crime 犯罪中止

(one who) discontinues a crime 中止犯
dismember the state 分裂国家
(crime of) disrupting marriage and the family 妨害婚姻、家庭（罪）
(crime of) disrupting the order of social administration 妨害社会管理秩序（罪）
disturb the social order 扰乱社会秩序
do not reform after repeated education 屡教不改
documentary evidence 书证

E

endanger society 危害社会
(crime of) endangering public security 危害公共安全（罪）
enticement 引诱
equal pay for equal work 同工同酬
escape 脱逃；逃跑
escape from prison 越狱逃跑
(act of) espionage 间谍（行为）
evade tax 偷税
evidence 证据
examination 检查
exculpation 辩解
execute a judgment 执行判决
execute a punishment 执行刑罚
execute (sentence) outside prison 监外执行（判决）
executing organ 执行机关
exempt from prosecution 免予起诉
exempt from (criminal) punishment 免除刑罚；免除处罚

expert evaluation　鉴定
expert witness　鉴定人
extort bribes　索贿
extort by blackmail　敲诈勒索
eyewitness　见证人

F

fabricate facts　捏造事实
facts of a crime　犯罪事实
false evidence or testimony　伪证
false proof　虚假证明
falsely accuse　诬告
falsely accuse and frame　诬（告）陷（害）
falsely pass off　假冒
falsify evidence　伪造证据
file a case　立案
final judgment　终审的判决
find guilty (not guilty)　认定有（无）罪
fine　罚金
first instance (case of), (judgment of), (procedure of)　第一审（案件），（判决），（程序）
fixed-term imprisonment　有期徒刑
forcibly seize　抢夺
forge official documents　伪造公文
frame　陷害
freedom of correspondence　通信自由
freedom of religious belief　宗教信仰自由
fugitive　在逃
funds (articles) received as bribes　赃款（物）

G

general provisions 总则
give a bribe 行贿
give a heavier punishment 从重处罚
give a lesser punishment 从轻处罚
give a punishment beyond the maximum prescribed 加重处罚
give consideration according to the circumstances 酌情
give vent to spite or to retaliate 泄愤报复
go from place to place committing crimes 流窜作案
group that smuggles or speculates 走私，投机倒把集团
guardian 监护人
guilty 有罪
gun control regulations 枪支管理规定

H

habitual theft; habitually steal 惯窃
habitually swindle 惯骗
handle a case 办案
harbour criminal elements 窝藏犯罪分子
harmful consequences 损害结果；危害结果
hear (a case) 审理（案件）
hearing 审讯
high people's court 高级人民法院
hijack (airplanes, etc.) 劫持（飞机等）
hold in custody 羁押

hooligan activities 流氓活动
hooligan group 流氓集团
humiliate women 侮辱妇女

I

identify 指认
identity is unclear 身分不明
illegalities 违法情况
illegally chop down (trees) 盗伐（树木）
immunity 豁免权
implement 施行
impose a punishment 处刑
impose a sentence 判处
imprisonment 徒刑
incite 煽动
induce 诱骗
(crime of) infringing upon the rights of the person and the democratic rights of citizens 侵犯公民人身权利、民主权利（罪）
initiate public prosecution 提起公诉
injure people 伤人
(crime of) injury 伤害（罪）
innocent 无罪
innocent people 无罪的人
inspection 勘验
instigate 教唆；策动
instigator 教唆犯
insult human dignity 侮辱人格
intentional crime 故意犯罪
intentionally kill another 故意杀人

intermediate people's court　中级人民法院
interpreter　翻译人
interrogate; interrogation　讯问
intoxicated　醉酒
investigate　侦讯
investigate criminal responsibility　追究刑事责任
investigation　侦查；调查
investigation personnel　侦查人员
investigative experiment　侦查实验
investigatory activity　侦查活动
irresistible calamity　不能抗拒的灾祸
irresistible reasons　不能抗拒的原因

J

jailbreak　越狱
joint crime　共同犯罪
jointly commit rape in succession　共同轮奸
judge　审判员
judicial personnel　司法工作人员
jurisdiction　管辖

K

(crime of) killing another　杀人（罪）

L

law　法律
law-enforcement personnel　执法人员

laws and regulations on prison management 监管法规
laws and regulations on protection of cultural relics 保护文物法规
legal representative 法定代理人
legal system 法制
legally-prescribed punishment 法定刑
legally-prescribed time period 法定期间
legitimate defence 正当防卫
life imprisonment 无期徒刑
limitation 时效
live at home under surveillance 监视居住
lure 引诱；勾引

M

major suspect 重大嫌疑分子
make a formal apology 赔礼道歉
make a statement of repentance 具结悔过
make compensation for losses 赔偿损失
make restitution or pay compensation 退赔
mass rebellion 聚众叛乱
material evidence 物证
materials in the case file 案卷材料
maximum legally-prescribed punishment 法定最高刑
means of production 生产资料
mediation 调解
member of the armed forces in active service 现役军人
mental illness of an intermittant nature 间歇性精神病

mentally ill person　精神病人
minimum sentence　最低刑
minor　未成年人
misappropriate　挪用
mistaken complaint　错告
mitigated punishment　减轻处罚
monstrous crime　罪恶重大
most heinous crime　罪大恶极

N

narcotic　毒品
national border health and quarantine regulations　国境卫生检疫规定
neglect of duty　玩忽职守
negligence　过失
negligent crime　过失犯罪
negligently injure another　过失伤害他人
negligently kill another　过失杀人
(does) not agree with (a decision)　不服（判决）
notice　通知书

O

obtain a guarantor and await trial out of custody　取保候审
obtain evidence　调取证据
offend public morals　有伤风化
offender　人犯
open mail of one's own accord　私自开拆邮件

open the court session 开庭
opinion recommending prosecution 起诉意见书
order 裁定；责令；判令
orders and judgments that misuse the law 枉法裁判
organ of state power 国家权力机关

P

pardon 赦免
parole 假释
participant in proceedings 诉讼参与人
party 当事人
people's assessor 人民陪审员
people's court 人民法院
people's procuratorate 人民检察院
person directly responsible 直接责任人员
person serving (a document) 送达人
person undergoing rehabilitation through labour 劳教人员
petition 申诉
petitioner 申诉人
place emphasis on evidence and investigative research 重证据，重调查研究
place of reform through labour 劳动改造场所
plaintiff 原告人
planned supply coupons 计划供应票证
policy 政策
pornographic book 淫书
pornographic picture 淫画
pose as 冒充
postponement of the hearing 延期审理

preparation for a crime 犯罪预备
preparatory examination 预审
(one who) prepares for a crime 预备犯
(be) present at the scene to supervise 临场监督
(be) present in court 到庭
president of a chamber 庭长
president of the court 院长
principal offender 主犯
principal punishment 主刑
prison 监狱
prison raid 劫狱
private affairs 阴私
private prosecution 自诉
private prosecutor 自诉人
probation period 考验期限
probation period for suspension of sentence 缓刑考验期限
procedural activities 诉讼活动
procedural document 诉讼文件
procedural rights 诉讼权利
procuratorial committee 检察委员会
(conduct) procuratorial work 检查
pronounce a judgment 宣告判决
property 财产
property owned by the whole people 全民所有的财产
property collectively owned by the labouring masses 劳动群众集体所有的财产
(crime of) property violation 侵犯财产（罪）
prosecute 追诉
prosecution 起诉
prostitution 卖淫

protect criminals 包庇罪犯
protection of secrets 保密
protest 抗诉
protested case 抗诉案件
public construction 公共建设
public property 公共财产
public prosecution 公诉
public prosecutor 公诉人
public security organ 公安机关
public security station 公安派出所
public service 公务
punish 判刑；处罚
punishment 刑罚
pursue for arrest 追捕
pursue for arrest and bring to justice 追捕归案

Q

quash a case 撤销案件
quash the original judgment 撤销原判
question 询问；审问
(put) questions to 发问

R

rape 强奸
(commit) rape in succession 轮奸
recidivist 累犯
reconsideration 复议

record 记录
recorder 记录人
recover 追缴
reduce the sentence 减刑
reexamination 复查
reform through labour 劳动改造
reform-through-labour organ 劳动改造机关
rehabilitation through labour 劳动教养
reinspection 复验
reject 驳回
release 释放
release certificate 释放证明
release from rehabilitation 解除教养
release upon the completion of one's term 期(刑)满释放
remain out of custody and obtain medical treatment 保外就医
repent 悔改
report a case 报案
reprimand 训诫
resell 倒卖
resist arrest 抗拒逮捕
resist tax 抗税
review 复核；审查
revoke a parole 撤销假释
right to defence 辩护权
right to elect 选举权
right to be elected 被选举权
rights of the person 人身权利
ringleader 首要分子
rise in rebellion 叛乱
robbery 抢劫

S

scene of a crime 犯罪现场
seal up (property, etc.) 封存；查封（财产等）
search 搜查
search warrant 搜查证
second instance (case of), (judgment of), (procedure of) 第二审（案件），（判决），（程序）
secretly cross the national borders 偷越国境
secretly gather intelligence 刺探情报
security administration personnel 治安管理工作人员
seek exorbitant profits 牟取暴利
seize (property) 扣押（财产）
seize and deliver to the public security organ 扭送公安机关
self-seeking misconduct 徇私舞弊
sentence 判刑
sentence to... 判处……
(in addition) (exclusively) sentence to... （并）（单）处……
sentencing 量刑
sentencing standards 量刑标准
serious injury 重伤
service 送达
service certificate 送达证
(have) sexual relations with a young girl 奸淫幼女
shelter and rehabilitate 收容教养
shooting 枪决
small character poster 小字报
smuggle 走私
socialist legal system 社会主义法制
sorcerer 神汉

special amnesty decree 特赦令
special people's court 专门人民法院
special provisions 分则
speculation 投机倒把
speculative arbitrage 套汇
spread poison 投（放）毒（物）
state organ 国家机关
state personnel 国家工作人员
state secret 国家机密
statement 陈述；供述；供词
statement of defendant 被告人供述
steal 盗窃
steal and export 盗运出口
steal intelligence 窃取情报
stir up fights and cause trouble 寻衅滋事
subject matter of a case 案由
subject to discipline 管教
subject to surveillance 看管
subpoena 传票
subvert the government 颠覆政府
summon 传唤
summon for detention 拘传
superstitious sects and secret societies 会道门
supervise and control offenders 监管人犯
supplementary civil action 附带民事诉讼
supplementary investigation 补充侦查
supplementary punishment 附加刑
supreme people's court 最高人民法院
suspect 嫌疑分子
suspension of execution 缓期执行
suspension of sentence 缓刑
swindle 诈骗

system in which the second instance is the final instance 两审终审制

T

take advantage of one's office 利用职务
take facts as the basis and the law as the criterion 以事实为根据，以法律为准绳
take part in adjudication 陪审
term of the sentence 刑期
termination of control 解除管制
testimony 证言
(use) the threat of violence （以）暴力相威胁
thwart 阻挠
time period 期间
transcript 笔录
transfer 移送
(crime of) treason 叛国(罪)
turn over 检交
turn traitor 叛国

U

undermine social order 破坏社会秩序
(crime of) undermining the socialist economic order 破坏社会主义经济秩序（罪）
unlawful detention 非法拘禁
unlawful infringement 不法侵害
urgent danger prevention 紧急避险

use public office for private gain 假公济私
use torture to coerce a statement 刑讯逼供

V

verification 查实
(there is) verified evidence 查证属实
verify the identity 验明正身
victim 被害人
(in) view of the public 示众
violate lawful rights 侵犯合法权利
violence 暴力
voluntary surrender 投案自首

W

wanted for arrest 通缉在案
wanted order 通缉令
witch 巫婆
withdraw a complaint 撤回告诉
withdraw from the court 退出法庭
withdraw prosecution 撤回起诉
withdrawal 回避
witness 证人
written decision 决定书
written judgment 判决书
written order 裁定书
written protest 抗诉书

汉英词汇对照表
CHINESE-ENGLISH GLOSSARY

A

案件　[anjian] case
案卷材料　[anjuan cailiao] materials in the case file
案情重大、复杂　[anqing zhongda, fuza] circumstances of a case are major or complex
案由　[anyou] subject matter of a case

B

办案　[ban'an] handle a case
包庇罪犯　[baobi zuifan] protect criminals
保护文物法规　[baohu wenwu fagui] laws and regulations on protection of cultural relics
保密　[baomi] protection of secrets
保外就医　[baowai jiuyi] remain out of custody and obtain medical treatment
暴力　[baoli] violence
（以）暴力相威胁　[(yi) baoli xiang weixie] (use) the threat of violence
爆炸　[baozha] cause explosions
报案　[bao'an] report a case
被告人　[beigaoren] defendant

被害人　[beihairen] victim
被选举权　[beixuanjuquan] right to be elected
笔录　[bilu] transcript
变造公文　[bianzao gongwen] alter official documents
辩护　[bianhu] defence
辩护律师　[bianhu lüshi] defence lawyer
辩护权　[bianhuquan] the right to defence
辩护人　[bianhuren] defender
辩解　[bianjie] exculpation
并处　[bingchu] in addition sentence to ...
驳回　[bohui] reject
剥夺政治权利　[boduo zhengzhi quanli] deprivation of political rights
补充侦查　[buchong zhencha] supplementary investigation
不法侵害　[bufa qinhai] unlawful infringement
不服（判决）　[bufu (panjue)] does not agree (with a decision)
不能抗拒的原因　[buneng kangjude yuanyin] irresistible reasons
不能抗拒的灾祸　[buneng kangjude zaihuo] irresistible calamity
不轻信口供　[buqingxin kougong] credence should not be readily given to oral statements

C

裁定　[caiding] order
裁定书　[caidingshu] written order
财产　[caichan] property

财物 [caiwu] article of property
残害耕畜 [canhai gengchu] cruelly injure or slaughter draft animals
策动 [cedong] instigate
查封（财产等） [chafeng (caichan deng)] seal up (property, etc.)
查获 [chahuo] apprehend
查实 [chashi] verification
查证属实 [chazheng shushi] (there is) verified evidence
撤回告诉 [chehui gaosu] withdraw a complaint
撤回起诉 [chehui qisu] withdraw prosecution
撤销案件 [chexiao anjian] quash a case
撤销假释 [chexiao jiashi] revoke a parole
撤销原判 [chexiao yuanpan] quash the original judgment
陈述 [chenshu] statement
惩办与宽大相结合 [chengban yü kuanda xiangjiehe] combine punishment with leniency
持械聚众叛乱 [chijie juzhong panluan] armed mass rebellion
重婚 [chonghun] bigamy
重新犯罪 [chongxin fanzui] commit a new crime
重新审判 [chongxin shenpan] new adjudication
出庭 [chuting] appear in court
处罚 [chufa] punish
处刑 [chuxing] impose a punishment
传唤 [chuanhuan] summon
传票 [chuanpiao] subpoena
串供 [chuan'gong] collude with others to devise a consistent story
刺探情报 [citan qingbao] secretly gather intel-

ligence
从犯 [congfan] accomplice
从轻处罚 [congqing chufa] give a lesser punishment
从重处罚 [congzhong chufa] give a heavier punishment
错告 [cuogao] mistaken complaint

D

打、砸、抢 [da, za, qiang] beat, smash and loot
大字报 [dazibao] big character poster
逮捕 [daibu] arrest
逮捕证 [daibuzheng] arrest warrant
单处 [danchu] exclusively sentence to ...
当事人 [dangshiren] party
倒卖 [daomai] resell
到庭 [daoting] be present in court
盗伐（树木） [daofa (shumu)] illegally chop down (trees)
盗窃 [daoqie] steal
盗运出口 [daoyun chukou] steal and export
第二审（案件）、（判决）、（程序） [diershen (anjian), (panjue), (chengxu)] second instance (case of), (judgment of), (procedure of)
第一审（案件）、（判决）、（程序） [diyishen (anjian), (panjue), (chengxu)] first instance (case of), (judgment of), (procedure of)
颠覆政府 [dianfu zhengfu] subvert the government
调查 [diaocha] investigation
调取证据 [diaoqu zhengju] obtain evidence
定案 [ding'an] determine a case

定罪 [dingzui] determine a crime
斗殴 [dou'ou] brawl
毒品 [dupin] narcotic
独立适用 [duli shiyong] apply (a punishment) in an independent manner
渎职（罪） [duzhi (zui)] (crime of) dereliction of duty

F

发问 [fawen] put questions to
罚金 [fajin] fine
法定代理人 [fading dailiren] legal representative
法定期间 [fading qijian] legally-prescribed time period
法定刑 [fading xing] legally-prescribed punishment
法定最高刑 [fading zuigao xing] maximum legally prescribed punishment
法令 [faling] decree
法律 [falü] law
法制 [fazhi] legal system
翻译人 [fanyiren] interpreter
反革命（罪） [fan'geming (zui)] (crime of) counter-revolution
反革命分子 [fan'geming fenzi] counterrevolutionary element
反诉 [fansu] counterclaim
犯人 [fanren] criminal
犯罪 [fanzui] crime; commit a crime
犯罪分子 [fanzui fenzi] criminal element
犯罪活动 [fanzui huodong] criminal activity

犯罪集团　[fanzui jituan] criminal group
犯罪情节　[fanzui qingjie] circumstances of a crime
犯罪人　[fanzuiren] criminal
犯罪事实　[fanzui shishi] facts of a crime
犯罪未遂　[fanzui weisui] criminal attempt
犯罪嫌疑人　[fanzui xianyiren] criminal suspect
犯罪现场　[fanzui xianchang] scene of a crime
犯罪行为　[fanzui xingwei] criminal act
犯罪预备　[fanzui yubei] preparation for a crime
犯罪中止　[fanzui zhongzhi] discontinuation of crime
防险　[fangxian] danger prevention
妨害婚姻、家庭（罪）[fanghai hunyin, jiating (zui)] (crime of) disrupting marriage and the family
妨害社会管理秩序（罪）[fanghai shehui guanli zhixü (zui)] (crime of) disrupting the order of social administration
放火　[fanghuo] arson
非法拘禁　[feifa jujin] unlawful detention
诽谤　[feibang] defame; defamation
分裂国家　[fenlie guojia] dismember the state
分则　[fenze] special provisions
封存（财产等）　[fengcun (caichan deng)] seal up (property, etc.)
附带民事诉讼　[fudai minshi susong] supplementary civil action
附加适用　[fujia shiyong] apply (a punishment) in a supplementary manner
附加刑　[fujia xing] supplementary punishment
复查　[fucha] reexamination
复核　[fuhe] review
复验　[fuyan] reinspection
复议　[fuyi] reconsideration

G

改判 [gaipan] revise a judgment
高级人民法院 [gaoji renmin fayuan] high people's court
告诉 [gaosu] complain; bring a complaint
公安机关 [gong'an jiguan] public security organ
公安派出所 [gong'an paichusuo] public security station
公共财产 [gonggong caichan] public property
公共财物 [gonggong caiwu] article of public property
公共建设 [gonggong jianshe] public construction
公民私人所有的合法财产 [gongmin siren suoyoude hefa caichan] citizens' lawful privately-owned property
公诉 [gongsu] public prosecution
公诉案件 [gongsu anjian] case of public prosecution
公诉人 [gongsuren] public prosecutor
公务 [gongwu] public service
共同轮奸 [gongtong lunjian] jointly commit rape in succession
共同犯罪 [gongtong fanzui] joint crime
供词 [gongci] statement
供述 [gongshu] statement
勾结外国 [goujie waiguo] collude with foreign states
勾引 [gouyin] lure
故意犯罪 [guyi fanzui] intentional crime
故意杀人 [guyi sharen] intentionally kill another
拐卖人口 [guaimai renkou] abduct and sell people

拐骗　[guaipian] abduct
关押　[guanya] custody
管教　[guanjiao] subject to discipline
管辖　[guanxia] jurisdiction
管制　[guanzhi] control
惯窃　[guanqie] habitual theft; habitually steal
惯骗　[guanpian] habitually swindle
国家工作人员　[guojia gongzuo renyuan] state personnel
国家机关　[guojia jiguan] state organ
国家机密　[guojia jimi] state secret
国家权力机关　[guojia quanli jiguan] organ of state power
国境卫生检疫规定　[guojing weisheng jianyi guiding] national border health and quarantine regulations
过失　[guoshi] negligence
过失犯罪　[guoshi fanzui] negligent crime
过失杀人　[guoshi sharen] negligently kill another
过失伤害他人　[guoshi shanghai taren] negligently injure another

H

和解　[hejie] arrange a settlement
合议庭　[heyi ting] collegial panel
互相配合，互相制约　[huxiang peihe, huxiang zhiyue] coordinate with each other and restrain each other
缓期执行　[huanqi zhixing] suspension of execution
缓刑　[huanxing] suspension of sentence

缓刑考验期限 [huanxing kaoyan qixian] probation period for suspension of sentence
回避 [huibi] withdrawal
悔改 [huigai] repent
毁灭罪证 [huimie zuizheng] destroy criminal evidence
会道门 [huidaomen] superstitious sects and secret societies
贿赂 [huilu] bribe
豁免权 [huomian quan] immunity

J

基层人民法院 [jiceng renmin fayuan] basic people's court
羁押 [jiya] hold in custody
记录 [jilu] record
记录人 [jiluren] recorder
计划供应票证 [jihua gongying piaozheng] planned supply coupons
既遂犯 [jisuifan] one who consummates a crime
加重处罚 [jiazhong chufa] give a punishment beyond the maximum prescribed
假公济私 [jiagong jisi] use public office for private gain
假冒 [jiamao] falsely pass off
假释 [jiashi] parole
假药 [jiayao] bogus medicine
间谍行为 [jiandie xingwei] act of espionage
间歇性精神病 [jianxiexing jingshenbing] mental illness of an intermittent nature

监管法规　[jian'guan fagui] laws and regulations on prison management

监管人犯　[jian'guan renfan] supervise and control offenders

监护人　[jianhuren] guardian

监视居住　[jianshi juzhu] live at home under surveillance

监外执行　[jianwai zhixing] execute (sentence) outside prison

监狱　[jianyu] prison

奸淫幼女　[jianyin younü] have sexual relations with a young girl

检查　[jiancha] examination

检察　[jiancha] conduct procuratorial work; prosecute

检察长　[jianchazhang] chief procurator

检察委员会　[jiancha weiyuanhui] procuratorial committee

检交　[jianjiao] turn over

检举　[jianju] accuse

检举人　[jianjuren] accuser

检举失实　[jianju shishi] accusation at variance with the facts

减轻处罚　[jianqing chufa] mitigated punishment

减刑　[jianxing] reduce the sentence

见证人　[jianzhengren] eyewitness

鉴定　[jianding] expert evaluation

鉴定人　[jiandingren] expert witness

教唆　[jiaosuo] instigate

教唆犯　[jiaosuofan] instigator

劫持（飞机等）　[jiechi (feiji deng)] hijack (air-

planes, etc.)
劫狱 [jieyu] prison raid
解除管制 [jiechu guanzhi] termination of control
解除教养 [jiechu jiaoyang] release from rehabilitation
解剖 [jiepou] autopsy
界碑 [jiebei] boundary tablet
界桩 [jiezhuang] boundary marker
紧急避险 [jinji bixian] urgent danger prevention
精神病人 [jingshenbingren] mentally ill person
拘传 [juchuan] summon for detention
拘禁 [jujin] detain; detention
拘留 [juliu] detain; detention
拘留证 [juliuzheng] detention warrant
拘役 [juyi] criminal detention
具结悔过 [jujie huiguo] make a statement of repentance
聚众犯罪 [juzhong fanzui] assemble a crowd to commit a crime
聚众叛乱 [juzhong panluan] mass rebellion
决水 [jueshui] breach dikes
军火 [junhuo] ammunition
决定书 [juedingshu] written decision

K

开庭 [kaiting] open the court session
看管 [kan'guan] subject to surveillance
看守所 [kanshousuo] detention house
勘验 [kanyan] inspection
抗拒逮捕 [kangju daibu] resist arrest

抗税　[kangshui] resist tax
抗诉　[kangsu] protest
抗诉书　[kangsushu] written protest
抗诉案件　[kangsu anjian] protested case
考验期限　[kaoyan qixian] probation period
控告　[konggao] complain; bring a complaint
控告人　[konggaoren] complainant
扣押（财产）　[kouya (caichan)] seize (property)

L

滥伐森林　[lanfa senlin] denude forests
滥用职权　[lanyong zhiquan] abuse one's powers
劳动改造　[laodong gaizao] reform through labour
劳动改造场所　[laodong gaizao changsuo] place of reform through labour
劳动改造机关　[laodong gaizao jiguan] reform through labour organ
劳动教养　[laodong jiaoyang] rehabilitation through labour
劳动群众集体所有的财产　[laodong qunzhong jiti suoyoude caichan] property collectively owned by the labouring masses
劳改犯　[laogaifan] criminal undergoing reform through labour
劳教人员　[laojiao renyuan] person undergoing rehabilitation through labour
累犯　[leifan] recidivist
类似　[leisi] analogous
立案　[li'an] file a case

利用职务上的便利 [liyong zhiwushangde bianli] take advantage of one's office

两审终审制 [liangshen zhongshen zhi] system in which the second instance is the final instance

量刑 [liangxing] sentencing

量刑标准 [liangxing biaozhun] sentencing standards

临场监督 [linchang jiandu] be present at the scene to supervise

流窜作案 [liucuan zuo'an] go from place to place committing crimes

流氓活动 [liumang huodong] hooligan activities

流氓集团 [liumang jituan] hooligan group

轮奸 [lunjian] commit rape in succession

屡教不改 [lüjiao bugai] do not reform after repeated education

M

卖淫 [maiyin] prostitution

冒充 [maochong] pose as

免除处罚 [mianchu chufa] exempt from (criminal) punishment

免除刑罚 [mianchu xingfa] exempt from criminal punishment

免予起诉 [mianyu qisu] exempt from prosecution

免予起诉决定书 [mianyu qisu jueding shu] decision to exempt from prosecution

民主权利 [minzhu quanli] democratic rights

没收财产 [moshou caichan] confiscation of property

牟取暴利 [mouqu baoli] seek exorbitant profits

N

捏造事实 [niezao shishi] fabricate facts
扭送公安机关 [niusong gong'an jiguan] seize and deliver to the public security organ
虐待 [nuedai] abuse
挪用 [nuoyong] misappropriate

O

殴打 [ouda] beat

P

判处 [panchu] impose a sentence; sentence to ...
判决 [panjue] decide (by judgment)
判决书 [panjueshu] written judgment
判令 [panling] order
判刑 [panxing] punish; sentence
叛国 [pan'guo] turn traitor
叛国（罪） [pan'guo (zui)] (crime of) treason
叛乱 [panluan] rise in rebellion
陪审 [peishen] take part in adjudication
赔偿损失 [peichang sunshi] make compensation for losses
赔礼道歉 [peili daoqian] make a formal apology
评议 [pingyi] deliberation
破坏行为 [pohuai xingwei] act of sabotage
破坏社会秩序 [pohuai shehui zhixu] undermine social order

破坏社会主义经济秩序（罪） [pohuai shehuizhuyi jingji zhixu (zui)] (crime of) undermining the socialist economic order

Q

欺骗 [qipian] deception
期间 [qijian] time period
期满释放 [qiman shifang] release upon the completion of one's term
起诉 [qisu] prosecution
起诉书 [qisushu] bill of prosecution
起诉意见书 [qisu yijianshu] opinion recommending prosecution
枪决 [qiangjue] shooting
枪支管理规定 [qiangzhi guanli guiding] gun control regulations
强奸 [qiangjian] rape
强制措施 [qiangzhi cuoshi] coercive measure
抢夺 [qiangduo] forcibly seize
抢劫 [qiangjie] robbery
敲诈勒索 [qiaozha lesuo] extort by blackmail
窃取情报 [qiequ qingbao] steal intelligence
侵犯财产（罪） [qinfan caichan (zui)] (crime of) property violation
侵犯合法权利 [qinfan hefa quanli] violate lawful rights
侵犯公民人身权利、民主权利（罪） [qinfan gongmin renshen quanli, minzhu quanli (zui)] (crime of) infringing upon the rights of the person and the democratic rights of citizens
情节 [qingjie] circumstances

驱逐出境 [quzhu chujing] deportation
取保候审 [qubao houshen] obtain a guarantor and await trial out of custody
全民所有的财产 [quanmin suoyoude caichan] property owned by the whole people

R

扰乱社会秩序 [raoluan shehui zhixu] disturb the social order
人犯 [renfan] offender
人民法院 [renmin fayuan] people's court
人民检查院 [renmin jianchayuan] people's procuratorate
人民陪审员 [renmin peishenyuan] people's assessor
人身权利 [renshen quanli] rights of the person
人身侮辱行为 [renshen wuru xingwei] act that subjects one's person to indignity
认定有（无）罪 [rending you(wu)zui] find guilty (not guilty)
肉刑 [rouxing] corporal punishment

S

杀人（罪） [sharen (zui)] (crime of) killing another
伤害（罪） [shanghai (zui)] (crime of) injury
伤人 [shangren] injure people
煽动 [shandong] incite
上诉 [shangsu] appeal
上诉案件 [shangsu anjian] appealed case
上诉状 [shangsuzhuang] appeal petition

社会主义法制 [shehuizhuyi fazhi] socialist legal system
赦免 [shemian] pardon
身份不明 [shenfen buming] identity is unclear
申诉 [shensu] petition
申诉人 [shensuren] petitioner
神汉 [shenhan] sorcerer
审查 [shencha] review
审理（案件） [shenli (anjian)] hear (a case)
审判 [shenpan] adjudicate; adjudication
审判委员会 [shenpan weiyuanhui] adjudication committee
审问 [shenwen] question
审讯 [shenxun] hearing
审判员 [shenpanyuan] judge
审判长 [shenpanzhang] chief judge
生产资料 [shengchan ziliao] means of production
生效 [shengxiao] become effective
尸体 [shiti] corpse
施行 [shixing] implement
时效 [shixiao] limitation
释放 [shifang] release
释放证明 [shifang zhengming] release certificate
示众 [shizhong] (in) view of the public
收件人 [shoujianren] addressee
收容教养 [shourong jiaoyang] shelter and rehabilitate
首要分子 [shouyao fenzi] ringleader
受贿 [shouhui] accept a bribe
受理（案件） [shouli (anjian)] accept (a case)
书记员 [shujiyuan] clerk
书证 [shuzheng] documentary evidence

数罪并罚 [shuzui bingfa] combined punishment for more than one crime
私自开拆邮件 [sizi kaichai youjian] open mail of one's own accord
司法工作人员 [sifa gongzuo renyuan] judicial personnel
死刑 [sixing] death penalty; death sentence
死刑缓期执行 [sixing huanqi zhixing] death penalty with a suspension of execution
搜查 [soucha] search
搜查证 [souchazheng] search warrant
送达 [songda] service
送达人 [songdaren] person serving (a document)
送达证 [songdazheng] service certificate
索贿 [suohui] extort bribes
诉讼参与人 [susong canyuren] participant in proceedings
诉讼活动 [susong huodong] procedural activities
诉讼权利 [susong quanli] procedural rights
诉讼文件 [susong wenjian] procedural document
损害 [sunhai] damage
损害结果 [sunhai jieguo] harmful consequences
损毁 [sunhui] damage

T

贪污（罪） [tanwu (zui)] (crime of) corruption
贪污公共财物 [tanwu gonggong caiwu] corruption involving articles of public property
坦白承认（罪行） [tanbai chengren (zuixing)] confess and acknowledge (one's crimes)

逃跑　[taopao] escape
套汇　[taohui] speculative arbitrage
特赦令　[tesheling] special amnesty decree
提起公诉　[tiqi gongsu] initiate a public prosecution
提请批准逮捕书　[tiqing pizhun daibu shu] application for approval of arrest
提审　[tishen] bring up and adjudicate (a case)
体罚　[tifa] corporal punishment
调解　[tiaojie] mediation
庭长　[tingzhang] president of a chamber
通缉令　[tongjiling] wanted order
通缉在案　[tongji zai'an] wanted for arrest
通谋　[tongmou] conspire
通信自由　[tongxin ziyou] freedom of correspondence
通知书　[tongzhishu] notice
同工同酬　[tonggong tongchou] equal pay for equal work
同居　[tongju] cohabit
偷税　[toushui] evade tax
偷越国境　[touyue guojing] secretly cross the national borders
投案自首　[tou'an zishou] voluntarily surrender
投敌叛变　[toudi panbian] defect to the enemy and turn traitor
投（放）毒（物）　[tou(fang) du(wu)] spread poison
投机倒把　[touji daoba] speculation
徒刑　[tuxing] imprisonment
退出法庭　[tuichu fating] withdraw from the court
退赔　[tuipei] make restitution or pay compensation
脱逃　[tuotao] escape

W

外交特权　[waijiao tequan] diplomatic privilege
玩忽职守　[wanhu zhishou] neglect of duty
枉法裁判　[wangfa caipan] orders and judgments that misuse the law
危害　[weihai] endanger
危害公共安全（罪）　[weihai gonggong anquan (zui)] (crime of) endangering public security
危害结果　[weihai jieguo] harmful consequences
危害社会　[weihai shehui] endanger society
维持原判　[weichi yuanpan] affirm the original judgment
违法情况　[weifa qingkuang] illegalities
违禁品　[weijinpin] contraband
伪造公文　[weizao gongwen] forge official document
伪造国家货币　[weizao guojia huobi] counterfeit national currency
伪造有价证券　[weizao youjia zhengquan] counterfeit valuable securities
伪造证据　[weizao zhengju] falsify evidence
伪证　[weizheng] false evidence or testimony
未成年人　[weichengnianren] minor
窝藏犯罪分子　[wocang fanzui fenzi] harbour criminal elements
窝藏赃物　[wocang zangwu] conceal booty
巫婆　[wupo] witch
诬告　[wugao] falsely accuse
诬（告）陷（害）　[wu(gao) xian(hai)] falsely accuse and frame
侮辱妇女　[wuru funü] humiliate women

侮辱人格 [wuru renge] insult human dignity
无期徒刑 [wuqi tuxing] life imprisonment
无罪 [wuzui] innocent
无罪的人 [wuzuide ren] innocent people
武器 [wuqi] arms
物证 [wuzheng] material evidence

X

嫌疑分子 [xianyi fenzi] suspect
陷害 [xianhai] frame
现行犯 [xianxingfan] active criminal
现役军人 [xianyi junren] a member of the armed forces in active service
小字报 [xiaozibao] small character poster
胁迫 [xiepo] coerce
泄愤报复 [xiefen baofu] give vent to spite or to retaliate
泄露国家机密 [xielu guojia jimi] disclose state secrets
行贿 [xinghui] give a bribe
行政处分 [xingzheng chufen] administrative sanction
刑罚 [xingfa] criminal punishment
刑罚处罚 [xingfa chufa] criminal punishment
刑法 [xingfa] criminal law
刑满释放证 [xingman shifang zheng] certificate of completion of sentence and release
刑期 [xingqi] term of the sentence
刑事处分 [xingshi chufen] criminal sanction
刑事犯罪行为 [xingshi fanzui xingwei] criminal act
刑事诉讼 [xingshi susong] criminal procedure

刑事诉讼法 [xingshi susongfa] criminal procedure law

刑事责任 [xingshi zeren] criminal responsibility

刑讯逼供 [xingxun bigong] use torture to coerce a statement

虚假证明 [xujia zhengming] false testimony

宣告判决 [xuangao panjue] pronounce a judgment

宣告无罪 [xuangao wuzui] announcement of not guilty

选举权 [xuanjuquan] right to elect

寻衅滋事 [xunxin zishi] stir up fights and cause trouble

询问 [xunwen] question

徇私舞弊 [xunsi wubi] self-seeking misconduct

训诫 [xunjie] reprimand

讯问 [xunwen] interrogate; interrogation

Y

延期审理 [yanqi shenli] postponement of the hearing

验明正身 [yanming zhengshen] verify the identity

移送 [yisong] transfer

以事实为根据，以法律为准绳 [yi shishi wei genju, yi falü wei zhunsheng] take facts as the basis and the law as the criterion

淫画 [yinhua] pornographic picture

淫书 [yinshu] pornographic book

引诱 [yinyou] lure; enticement

阴私 [yinsi] private affairs

隐匿罪证 [yinni zuizheng] conceal criminal evidence

优抚 [youfu] care for disabled servicemen and the families of revolutionary martyrs and servicemen
有悔罪表现 [you huizui biaoxian] demonstrate repentance
有立功表现 [you ligong biaoxian] demonstrate meritorious service
有期徒刑 [youqi tuxing] fixed-term imprisonment
有伤风化 [youshang fenghua] offend public morals
有罪 [youzui] guilty
又聋又哑的人 [youlong youyade ren] deaf-mute
诱骗 [youpian] induce
预备犯 [yubeifan] one who prepares for a crime
预审 [yushen] preparatory examination
原告人 [yuangaoren] plaintiff
院长 [yuanzhang] president of the court
越狱 [yueyu] jailbreak
越狱逃跑 [yueyu taopao] escape from prison

Z

在逃 [zaitao] fugitive
赃款（物） [zangkuan(wu)] funds (articles) received as bribes
赃物 [zangwu] booty
责令 [zeling] order
诈骗 [zhapian] swindle
招摇撞骗 [zhaoyao zhuangpian] cheat and bluff
侦查 [zhencha] investigation
侦查活动 [zhencha huodong] investigatory activity
侦查人员 [zhencha renyuan] investigation personnel
侦察实验 [zhencha shiyan] investigative experi-

ment

侦讯 [zhenxun] investigate

正当防卫 [zhengdang fangwei] legitimate defence

证据 [zhengju] evidence

证人 [zhengren] witness

证言 [zhengyan] testimony

政策 [zhengce] policy

直接责任人员 [zhijie zeren renyuan] person directly responsible

执法人员 [zhifa renyuan] law-enforcement personnel

执行 [zhixing] carry out; execute

执行机关 [zhixing jiguan] executing organ

执行判决 [zhixing panjue] execute a judgment

执行刑罚 [zhixing xingfa] execute a punishment

指认 [zhiren] identify

治安管理工作人员 [zhi'an guanli gongzuo renyuan] security administration personnel

致人伤残 [zhiren shangcan] cause a person's injury or disability

致人重伤（死亡） [zhiren zhongshang (siwang)] cause serious injury (death) to a person

质证 [zhizheng] cross-examination

中级人民法院 [zhongji renmin fayuan] intermediate people's court

中止犯 [zhongzhifan] one who discontinues a crime

终审的判决 [zhongshende panjue] final judgment

重大嫌疑分子 [zhongda xianyi fenzi] major suspect

重伤 [zhongshang] serious injury

重证据，重调查研究 [zhong zhengju, zhong diaocha

词汇对照表

yanjiu] place emphasis on evidence and investigative research

主犯　[zhufan] principal offender

主刑　[zhuxing] principal punishment

注销户口　[zhuxiao hukou] cancel one's residence registration

专门人民法院　[zhuanmen renmin fayuan] special people's court

追捕　[zhuibu] pursue for arrest

追捕归案　[zhuibu gui'an] pursue for arrest and bring to justice

追缴　[zhuijiao] recover

追究刑事责任　[zhuijiu xingshi zeren] investigate criminal responsibility

追诉　[zhuisu] prosecute

酌情　[zhuoqing] give consideration according to the circumstances

资敌　[zidi] aid an enemy

自首　[zishou] voluntary surrender

自诉　[zisu] private prosecution

自诉案件　[zisu anjian] case of private prosecution

自诉人　[zisuren] private prosecutor

宗教信仰自由　[zongjiao xinyang ziyou] freedom of religious belief

总则　[zongze] general provisions

纵容　[zongrong] connive at

走私　[zousi] smuggle

走私、投机倒把集团　[zousi, touji daoba jituan] group that smuggles or speculates

阻挠　[zu'nao] thwart

最低刑　[zuidi xing] minimum sentence
最高人民法院　[zuigao renmin fayuan] Supreme People's Court
罪大恶极　[zuida eji] most heinous crime
罪恶重大　[zui'e zhongda] monstrous crime
罪犯　[zuifan] criminal
罪名　[zuiming] charge
罪证　[zuizheng] criminal evidence
醉酒　[zuijiu] intoxicated

中 华 人 民 共 和 国 刑 法
中华人民共和国刑事诉讼法
*
外文出版社出版
(中国北京百万庄路24号)
外文印刷厂印刷
中国国际图书贸易总公司
(中国国际书店)发行
北京399信箱
1984年(34开)第一版
编号:(英汉)6050—49
00155
6—EC—1817P